Harris Latchu was born in a small riverside village, Trinidad West Indies. At the age of five, the family was relocated to the town of Chaguanas on the west side of Trinidad where he completed his schooling. After gaining his Cambridge certificate and having passed the civil service exam, he became a customs officer at the age of eighteen. However, to fulfil his ambition to become an electronic chartered engineer he decided to come to England at the age of twenty on the assumption that university education was available to all commonwealth citizens. Little did he know that one had to be resident in the UK for three years before he could apply for a University Grant, which is where this saga begins.

I dedicate this book to my late parents, Reuben and Eunice, who always instilled into me the importance of education if you want to progress.

Harris Latchu

BEYOND THE DRAGON'S MOUTH TO THE LAND OF MILK AND MONEY

AUSTIN MACAULEY PUBLISHERS™

LONDON • CAMBRIDGE • NEW YORK • SHARJAH

A CIP catalogue record for this title is available from the British Library.

ISBN 9781398495166 (Paperback)
ISBN 9781398495173 (ePub e-book)

www.austinmacauley.com

First Published 2023
Austin Macauley Publishers Ltd®
1 Canada Square
Canary Wharf
London
E14 5AA

I wish to thank my wife, Margaret, for her encouragement to complete this work and for typing the manuscript.

Table of Contents

Introduction

The whole of Britain is on total lock down in the midst of the COVID-19 pandemic. Normal life has ceased to be of any relevance. During this time my mind turned to the previous 79 years of my life. Where did I come from, and what were my early childhood experiences? The more I thought about this I realised that my children and grandchildren had no idea of how my life had panned out. I wanted the future generations to know who I was from a more personal point of view than two dimensional photographs can ever portray. This started by putting random memories daily into a note book upon which I could draw for a biography of my life. Memories came thick and fast but not in chronological order.

I thought I would try by beginning with my earliest memories of life in a river-side village on the banks of the Caroni River in rural Trinidad. The population of village was about 50 persons consisting of about ten families and who were mostly farmers and indentured sugar cane workers whose forefathers came from India circa 1845 onwards.

When the British government decided to build a highway, the entire village was relocated. In my family were three older brothers, an older sister, then came myself followed by two younger sisters. I was about aged five at the time of the relocation.

The more my memories flooded in I realised that I needed to document it for future generations of my family who having being born in England had no idea of life in Trinidad, a tropical island tucked into the coast of Venezuela in the lesser Antilles of the Caribbean sea. My forefathers were brought there as indentured labours from Utter Pradesh in North Eastern India. They came by ship one of which was the S.S. Hereford via the Dragon's mouth strait into to docks of Port of Spain Trinidad. From whence I left Trinidad aged 20 in 1961 for a new life in England where it was thought that the streets were paved with gold. Initially in the early days of my life in England I found out the truth, as I later realised that nothing comes to you except by hard work to achieve one's dream of becoming a chartered engineer.

Chapter 1
East Indian Indentured
Labour in Trinidad

Between 1845 and 1917 a total of 143,000 Indians migrated to Trinidad under the system of Indian Indenture. Most of these indentured labourers came from the agricultural and labouring classes of the Uttar Pradesh and Behar regions of North Eastern India, with a comparatively small number being recruited from Bengal and various areas in South India.

My great-great-grandmother Mata Ojeeran was born in Calcutta in 1825. It is highly probable that she was amongst the first group of people to embark on the perilous journey to Trinidad to become indentured labourers on the S.S. Fatel Rozack arriving on the 13th of May 1845 or the S.S. Bangalore or the S.S. Duke of Bedford a year later via the straits of the Dragon's Mouth into the docks at Port of Spain Trinidad. She arrived in Trinidad according to the records with three young sons, one of whom was my great- grandfather, James Latchu. I am assuming that two of the boys she may have adopted when their parents died on route but we will never know for sure as out of the 1124 passengers 12 died on route on these particular ships. (See Indian immigrant ship list Fig 2) One of the boys was called Jamureth which could be according to Indian tradition of naming a son by his father's surname. The name Jamureth is likely to be of Muslim origin coming from as far as Afghanistan but my family came from a Hindu tradition and were converted to Christianity by Canadian missionaries. Today a church still stands in the village of Bamboo called the Latchu Memorial church in honour of my great grandfather who preached there. It was with tremendous pleasure that my wife and I were able to worship there during our time in Trinidad and on subsequent visits.

Approximately 85% of the immigrants were Hindus and 14% Muslims. Despite the trying conditions experienced under the indentured systems, about 90% of Indian immigrants chose at the end of the contracted period of indenture, to make Trinidad their permanent home. The predominant age group of the immigrants was 20–30 years and while most came as unmarried there were those who came as small family units. The debate surrounding the nature and workings of the system in India is multi-faceted and open-ended. A lot of ambiguity has marked the system especially during its first three decades of operation. These include the recruitment process in India, The British role in the impoverishment of nineteenth-century India – a main push factor of Indian indenture, whether or not the Indians were fully aware of the real nature and details of the journey upon which they were embarking and their level of awareness of the fact that they were leaving Indian soil possibly forever is questionable. Initially the journey from India to Trinidad averaged at about three months, but it became substantially shorter and less turbulent with opening of the Suez Canal in 1869.

Conditions on board the ships were cramped and depressing and there were frequent out breaks of such diseases as typhoid, dysentery and measles which lead to high mortality rates on some of the journeys. The first two decades of the system were highly experimental in nature, lacking in settled rules and conditions. However, there were two constant and central features of the system. Immigrants were contracted for long periods with a single employer and there were penal sanctions for breach of the contract. On arrival in Trinidad the indentured immigrants were quarantined on Nelson Island and then assigned to the various estates for the contracted period; this was followed by a two year period which completed the industrial residence of five years. At the end of this five year period they were given freedom papers certifying that the individuals were no longer under indenture.

They had a choice of returning to India or staying and given ten acres of land to cultivate. My forefathers chose to remain and build a new life for themselves and start family life.

Chapter 2
Childhood Memories

When the ships arrived at the docks in Port of Spain, families were allocated to various parts of the sugar plantation areas in the colony. My forefathers were sent to the ward of Caroni and settled in a little village called Bejucal on the banks of the Caroni River. This was about 1890. My great- great grandmother arrived with three sons who were probably born on or boarded the ship S.S. Hereford in India. The surnames on the manifest were Latchu, Jaleel and Jamareth. My grandmother was registered as Ojera but there was no mention of her husband. After they had served their five years of indenture-ship, they all chose to remain in Trinidad and were each given ten acres of land near Bejucal. James Latchu, my grandfather married Elizabeth whose forefathers were probably from the same village in India and her parents were probably from the group of friends on board the ship S.S. Hereford. James my grandfather begat two sons and five daughters and his youngest child a son, Reuben, was my father. The Canadian missionaries spread the Christian Gospel in the various East Indian settlements and my grandfather was converted. He became a lay preacher in the Presbyterian Church in the village. A church was built in his memory in the relocated areas after the village was moved to facilitate the construction of a highway. The 'Latchu Memorial Church' still exists today in Bamboo village. My family and I have returned to the church to worship on several occasions.

I was five years old when my family of three brothers and three sisters moved to Chaguanas the rest of the families from Bejucal moved to Bamboo village. The reason my father chose to move to Chaguanas was because there were schools, medical centres, shops and a market. My father was a taxi driver and my mother was a house wife with very little education but plenty of wisdom. However, she was the driving force ensuring that we had a good education which has proved to be a way for us all to advance.

I was sent to the local school built by the British Government which was a primary school where the curriculum was based on the English system so all the books and rhymes did not necessarily relate to life in the tropics! For example, we sang songs like *Hickory Dickory Dock* and *Jack and Jill went up the Hill* also *Round and Round the Mulberry bush on a Cold and Frosty morning*! (What was 'frost', we had no idea!) The school was about two miles away from our house, and I walked there with my brothers (sometime barefooted!) but we always had a packed lunch consisting of a roti with a filling of curried potato and wrapped in a piece of cloth. In the morning period, we had free milk which was very welcome. One of my unpleasant memories of primary school was the periodic administration of Chinapodium (a worming medication) followed by a dose of Epsom salts, then we were sent home for the day. My education was interrupted for at least a year when I contracted osteomyelitis in my right foot, and I was hospitalised for a period of time. The operation on my foot created very deep scars and I was left with a limp. This disability made me very self-conscious, and sometimes I was belittled and called names. I believe this gave me the impetus to prove that I was as good as my friends or even better. The way forward was to maximise on my education and make something of myself. This had its drawback in that I was separated from my friends who chose to be carpenters or bricklayers and were transported by bus to another school.

At age ten, I was sent to my Uncle Isaac's to further my primary schooling and also help him in his shop which sold not only provisions but also alcohol. Sometimes I manned the shop even serving alcoholic drinks in the so-called 'Rum Shop'. I can remember having to stand on a box to reach the counter and to use the weighing scales. In my opinion, this is where I developed my skills for numbers as in those days there were no calculators or tills which calculated the right change so one had to do all the sums in one's own head. I did not enjoy at that time very much because after school instead of playing football or cricket I had to mind the shop including weekends, and even Sundays. I did not have any friends or belong to any clubs, and I very often requested to be taken back home, but this was refused on the grounds that I was there to help my uncle and also there was one less mouth to feed.

My uncle was a contractor to build roads, and he had a shed in which he kept all his tools. As I did not have any toys, I would very often borrow the tools to make my own toy including a scooter with ball-baring wheels, and I even attempted to build a car which consisted of a grocery box copying the design of a neighbour's child's peddle car. It was a very ambitious project, and I almost lost a finger from using a sharp saw. There was no TV or radio or even electricity. Our lighting was from gas lamps, and one of my jobs before dark was to pump up the pressure in the gas cylinder to ignite the gas which produced a glow to the mantle. The mantle became very brittle and any rough handling would have caused it to disintegrate so I had to be very careful. Needless to say I had many accidents and bruises from my uncle's hand. On occasional weekends, I was allowed to go home to my parents which I looked forward to very much for several reasons one of which was to reunite with my guard dog Samson who was very fond of me because one of my jobs was to feed him left-over rice. Another reason was that I was able go and play football and cricket and fly kites on windy days. Sadly I was taken back on Sunday evening in time for school and my job in the shop. I stayed with my uncle until I finished primary school and my mother in her wisdom thought that I would be better off at home as the secondary school run by Catholic fathers was in the local town. This was a fee paying school, and it was quite a burden on my parents financially as my other siblings were also at secondary school one of which was a boarding school. Luckily my eldest brother Harold was also a bread winner because he became a tailor so was also able to help with our education and also sew clothes for us. My father's taxi business was also doing okay and that also helped with our education. I continued to have important chores including responsibilities for cleaning the lamp shades, from the soot produced by the kerosene, before sunset at 6 pm, which it always does in the tropics. Unfortunately at that time our cricket game or football matches were at the crucial point and it was very irritating for me to be called away to do the lamps. This job continued until we had electricity in the town. My other chore was to provide dry wood for cooking on the chulha (an Indian oven with a domed top). This was a very important job. First of all I had to select really dry wood so that not much smoke would be produced. Ignition was aided with the use of a pukkni (Indian style blow tube used like bellows). This continued until we obtained a kerosene stove. The wood was obtained from the mangrove swamp near the Caroni River. I used to go with my father to collect it in his boat. I was rewarded with an hour of fishing which was the ploy used by my father to go.

My father gave up his job as a taxi driver and bought a van to become a market trader. He would go to the main market in Port of Spain to purchase fruit and vegetables and resell them at a profit in the local market in our town. I was often taken with him on Friday night to guard the purchases as he bartered individually. We would leave for the market about 3 am to set up a stall in the local market. Stalls were allocated on a first come first served basis so we had to be early to get a good spot. I assisted my father all day Saturday and my mother who also joined us there. I would get money from my father to do the weekly meat shopping in the meat section of the market run by the local farmers who butchered their livestock for local consumption. We would always have beef or goat meat for dinner on Saturday and any vegetables or fruit left over unsold like avocados, sweet potatoes, bananas, melon, tomatoes or cucumbers we took home; this ensured that we always had food on the table for the rest of the week.

On Sunday, we usually had a duck or chicken or occasionally turkey from our home flock of poultry.

Another of my jobs was to mind and operate the rice mill we owned; that was another commercial venture my father had, and it was very successful. He first of all purchased it to grind the rice he harvested in our own paddy field but then opened it up for the local farmers who paid for the service, and the husks were sold for chicken feed or pig food. The paddy fields were in the village, from whence our family was relocated, on the banks of the Caroni River. The process of faming rice is in various stages which included ploughing the land and preparing for planting in the wet season. The latter was done when the paddy fields were flooded by rain and the opening of sluice gates to prevent flooding from the river. The nursery plants grown from seed were planted into the ground which was knee deep in water. The farmers often helped each other and I was often recruited to plant. It was a messy job especially when we had to remove weeds to increase the yield. I would accompany my mother to do this chore and I invariably ended up covered in mud on my legs which caked up in the tropical sun when we stopped for lunch. This was a cherished time with my mother as she so appreciated my help, and we would talk about many things and how fortunate we were to have this land which produced enough rice for the family for a whole year. Rice being the staple diet and was eaten every day. My father was also grateful for my effort because he was able to provide food for his seven children. Some of the rice was sold in the market after being dried and milled to remove the husks. When the wet green rice was bought in before it could be stored, it had to be dried and the chaff removed by winnowing it. I would often climb on a stool to get some height and as the wind picked up I separated the chaff from the grain and then dried. I often found myself whistling for wind because when you are working in 90 degrees heat any delay in completing that task was very uncomfortable.

It was not all work as I also had plenty time to play during my childhood days. In spite of the disability of my right foot, I was reasonably good at football and was always put in centre forward position. Our Club 'Young Defenders' did fairly well in the competitions, and I was a key and somewhat popular member of the club. I was fairly good at cricket and was always the opening batsman but did not excel unlike one of my brothers who represented our country against a visiting team. I spent many happy hours kite flying in the local park and was very skilful at making my own kites because I had the foresight to use materials found at home. First of all I used brown grocery bags then I reinforced the shape of the kite with the centre stem of a coconut leaf described as being like the spinal cord running down the centre of the main leaf. The tail of the kite was made from rags of old clothes. The string was gathered from the threads used to sew flour bags but occasionally I would steal thread from my brothers tailoring business. I paid heavily if I got caught! Another of my hobbies was playing marbles and very often competing against my friends using buttons taken from discarded trousers and sometimes from my own trousers or shirt for prizes. I was also skilful at table tennis and our home was often full of my young friends as we had our own table tennis table. My older brother who was not as good as me was a bad loser and he would threaten to hit me but I could run faster than him so escaped!

Chapter 3
My Education and Aspirations

English was the official language of instruction in Trinidad and Tobago in primary and secondary schools to facilitate communication across the country's several language groups. Education was compulsory for children between 6–12 years old and primary where children 5–11 years old were enrolled including two primary grades (infants) and five standard grades (junior). Further education of the secondary schooling was divided between two cycles, a first cycle lasting five years for children 11–16 years of age for which graduates received the Cambridge secondary education certificate equivalent to GCSE and a second cycle lasting two years where graduates received GCSE advanced level. Higher education was provided through a variety of institutions including the University of the West Indies.

My ambition has always been since an early age to be an engineer and in particular electronic and electrical engineering. I completed my primary education with promising results. From 1954–59, I was a pupil at the college of St Philips and St James where I began my 'sound colonial' education. This consisted the English curriculum of English, mathematics, history, geography but no science subjects. This somewhat had a detrimental effect on my dreams of an engineering career; nevertheless I concentrated on the science requirements.

Even though I was never in the top group in my secondary education, I excelled in mathematics and English and eventually I obtained a 2nd grade in the Cambridge certificate. This achievement had a significant effect on the direction my life and career would take. Most of my friends in my group only got a 3rd grade certificate which entitled them to a career in teaching. However a 2nd grade was required to have a career in the Civil Service for which a further exam was required. A good knowledge of the British constitution was needed so I swatted up a great deal on the names of the government officials and British law.

I did well in this examination, and I applied to join the civil service in 1959. I was appointed a job as a customs officer.

During this period of employment I still had the dream of becoming an engineer but I was aware that I required advanced level in mathematics and a science subject. I proceeded to do part time study at Queen Mary's college in Port of Spain which was near where I was employed at the docks. This was not a very happy time for me because I lost contact with most of my friends who chose other careers in teaching, pharmacy and working in the law courts or administration posts in the sugar industry. At that time, the only way to get further education including university one was that you had to be from a rich privileged family to do a degree. I made the decision to go to England where I heard that if you had the entry requirements university education was free. During that time the British Government were recruiting nurses and there were no restrictions on entering the UK as I was a British citizen. I did some serious thinking on my situation and had to decide to continue my employment with the civil service or migrate to England and achieve my ambition to become an engineer. At the age of 20 years old, I decided to resign from my job to many people's surprise, and even though I did not complete my A level education I booked a single ticket on the S.S. Southern Cross bound for England in August 1961.

On the ship were a number of people from Australia and New Zealand also other colonies of the UK who were either migrating or going on holiday. Also on the ship were those either recruited by the British council for nursing or labourers for the building industries or to work on the buses and trains. I was initially put in the first class section of the ship for the reason of my status as an ex-customs officer whilst the other immigrants were on the lower decks in 4 berth cabins. This was not a privilege as I was parted from my friends and countrymen. I was very uncomfortable for the first few days especially at meal times being presented with so many implements that I was totally unused to using also cultural differences such as drinking wine with dinner having three courses such as starters, main followed by pudding. The only time I had met the word 'pudding' was when we sang at primary school, *Georgy Porgy Pudding and Pie* which had no relevant meaning to me at that time. I also remembered how uncomfortable I was during breakfast time especially when I had to make a choice of having bacon and egg, or which cereal I would like. "A boiled egg," asked the waiter who called me 'sir'. An English man calling me sir was quite intimidating because before now he would have been my master in the

Caribbean like those who were employed by Tate & Lyle Sugars. Another time I ordered a boiled egg and two eggs were presented in eggcups and I vividly remembered the difficulty I had dealing with these two eggs as I had never had a whole boiled egg before and also I had lots of implements and I did not know which one to use. A chaplain on the same table saw my plight and asked are you a 'cutter' or a 'basher' which added to my confusion; what did he mean? He kindly explained to me how to deal with the eggs by either taking the spoon and bashing the top and then scooping out the egg or I could chop off the top with the knife to expose the yolk. I chose the knife method and thereafter I could now deal with boiled eggs. He also explained which implements to use and in which sequence. Thereafter I became more comfortable at mealtimes. I was invited to hang out with some of them and this was not an enjoyable experience as the language was different, the drinks were different from what I had had in the past and that is where I learnt to drink beer! I was even more uncomfortable when the priest became too friendly and invited me to his cabin and that is when I asked to be transferred to the same table as my friends.

The journey to England took about three weeks and I enjoyed the experience and made many friends with the people of the Caribbean one of whom I lived with for a while in the UK.

The journey on S.S. Southern Cross was a thousand times better than that my forefathers had on their journey from India all those years ago. On the ships, then they were kept below decks in cramped conditions. Disease was rife like cholera, typhoid and dysentery and quite a few died on route. In spite of the extreme hardship, my forefathers survived the voyage as the ship pulled into the beautiful harbour of Port of Spain via the strait of the Dragon's Mouth. My voyage was very much more comfortable and after 21 days at sea we sailed into Southampton Harbour on a very misty and cold morning in stark contrast to the warm and bright mornings of the Caribbean. We were very excited to get on deck to see what England looked like having heard so much about the 'Mother Land' where pavements were supposedly paved with gold. I was dressed as I would at home and as I was shivering the priest advised me to put on some warm clothing. I was not prepared for temperate climes and did not have any warm clothing so I returned to my warm cabin till disembarkation.

Chapter 4
My Arrival and Surprises

I arrived in the summer August 1961 at the port of Southampton in the early hours of the morning. I was eager to see what this green and pleasant land looked like. I was dressed in my tropical wear not expecting it to be cold, misty and damp. I was told that I should put on some warm clothing such as a jumper but I was a bit perplexed as I did not know what a jumper was! My first surprise was seeing white people doing manual jobs such as handling the baggage and even sweeping the dockside. I disembarked at 9 am to join a long queue of hopeful immigrants who came on the same ship who came from various Caribbean islands including Jamaica, Barbados, Grenada and Trinidad.

Most of the people were dressed in tropical style dress; the women wearing floral frocks and the men in suits and ties including myself. The custom officers did not look very friendly and the baggage handlers even less so. I felt a slight antagonism from the local people in seeing so many waves of immigrants coming to their country and no doubt taking their jobs and worsening the housing situation.

By then, the temperature had risen to about 20 degrees and it felt as though I was in a large air conditioned room. I liked this condition because only the very rich in Trinidad could afford air conditioning. In England, this was free and available to all! I was now in a temperate climate vastly different to the tropics which I left to seek my further education and to enjoy some of the so-called gold pavements; a major reason for leaving my homeland.

After collecting my luggage, one suitcase of which was crammed with tropical treats for my host and my sister who had been recruited by the British Council as a trainee nurse the year before. My host expected me to stay with him for a few days and then move on to my planned accommodation and work place as he had hosted my sister who was later accommodated at the Nurse's Home to carry on with nursing training. He was extremely surprised that I had no such plans and that I had chucked in my job as a customs officer in Trinidad, also his homeland as well which he had left two years previously, and was employed as a factory worker assembling radios and tape recorders for Fidelity Radio.

Nevertheless he took me to his home as a temporary measure and this was my second surprise. He lived in the attic of a three floor building owned by a Nigerian immigrant who also let the other floors to other immigrants. The attic was also occupied by his family and his brother's family. There were five of us in this two bedroom apartment which had no heating or hot water and the kitchen was on the landing. It had no cupboards just a gas cooker and a wash basin. I soon settled in that place because the people around me were from my own environment.

There was a further addition to the apartment when a fellow Trinidadian, came to stay during his summer vacation, and shared a room with me which led to the apartment being overcrowded. Additionally during the weekends our host's wife's sister, a trainee nurse and my sister would stay on their days off so we had in this two- bedroom flat nine adults and as far as I know the landlord either turned a blind eye or was unaware that it was so overcrowded. This house was in the west side of London where most West Indians settled. With no showering facilities, we often we had to use the local communal baths. That was an experience for me as in the Caribbean one showered at least once a day and also I had never been in a bathtub before. The procedure was at the bath house you were given a bar of soap and a towel and allowed 20 minutes to complete your bath because there was a long queue waiting to have their weekly bath. The bath cleaner, a white man, expressed his distaste when he had to clean off the grimy bath ring. He thought it was the black skin coming off the immigrant bathers!

As there were three families living in our house including the basement from Sri Lanka and the Nigerian landlord on the middle floor, there were three different types of cooking smell from hot Sri Lankan curry, pungent Nigerian stews and West Indian salt fish the latter being a favourite dish of Trinidad. On the second day of my arrival when I was getting acclimatised as it was fairly warm in August, my host agreed to take me on my first outing to visit the sights of London. I was very excited when he said we would take the tube from Ladbrook Grove via Oxford Circus to feed the pigeons in Trafalgar Square then he said we would finish the day seeing Buckingham Palace. I had never heard or seen what the tube television in Trinidad but I was excited that we would go to a circus and also see where the royal family lived.

My imagination was nothing like what it is as I imagined that it was an inflated rubber tube but not like a train. Oxford Circus was just a stop with not a big top in sight. I was immensely disappointed when I saw what Buckingham Palace looked like as I imagined; a large building with turrets and looking like a fairy tale castle, it was an ordinary building with security railings and soldiers marching up and down in front of the house. My host mentioned that because the flag was flying that the Queen was in residence. To my amazement Trafalgar Square was round but it was great to see lots of pigeons and I even bought pigeon feed from one of the many vendors to feed them. This delighted me because this is one of the photos my sister sent to our parents which I saw and thus I was able to do the same.

Needless to say during my first sight-seeing visit to London I was filled with reverential awe seeing the tall buildings and sky scrapers and the density of the multitudes of people of different nationalities and skin pigmentation milling around, the noisiness of the traffic including the red double decker buses and black taxi cabs. After all, I came from a village with minimal numbers of people and traffic so it was quite an experience as compared to my childhood environment. There were more first time experiences to come including my first taste of fish and chips for lunch and also the ease of getting around the city by bus and train. Even pavements were an experience as at home it was usually unpaved and dusty.

It was a long and exciting day and we ended up the day going to the cinema at Leicester Square and with yet another experience when we came out of the cinema at 10 pm it was still day light. In the tropics, darkness fell promptly at 6 pm.

Chapter 5
My First Two Years in England

It did not take me long to realise that I had not done my homework diligently before my decision to emigrate to England as I had made some assumptions that were unfounded like the ease of finding accommodation and employment and above all the free availability of higher education.

I soon learnt that the limited funds I had when I arrived were not sufficient to pay for full time education because to my horror you had to be resident for three years in the country before you could apply for university. I also realised that to get the necessary qualifications like A level in mathematics and physics I would have to go college on a full-time basis followed by three years at university to fulfil my ambition of becoming an engineer.

My hopes were dashed when I found out that none of this was possible and I would have to pay the necessary fees. Since I did not have the finance or financial backing from my parents or the Trinidad government the latter of which you would get only on a scholarship basis and my parents could not afford it, I had to do some serious decision making as to whether I should return to my homeland or persevere with my initial decision and stay come what may. Since I had burnt my bridges by resigning my secure job and also losing face by returning so shortly after leaving I decided that I had no choice but to remain in the UK and 'Do or Die'.

The honeymoon period ended abruptly, and I had to find employment and even more traumatic was to find accommodation. I applied for an office job thinking that with my GCE qualifications and recommendation from my past employer in Trinidad and that I came from the same village where the famous author V.S. Naipaul lived would bode me well, however none of the above testimonies helped.

I was never invited for interview for the at least three applications I had made. One of my applications resulted in a telephone interview when the interviewer soon realised by my accent that I was an immigrant and he posed questions like naming the major cities in the UK and where is Birmingham, which I could not answer as London was the only one I knew as I thought it was the only city in England. It was my first experience of prejudice even though I was well qualified for the job. The next experience of prejudice I had was in finding accommodation as my host had given me notice to leave in three weeks' time as he was moving to a different flat and he would not be able to accommodate me. However my host arranged for me to have an interview at the factory where he was employed and I was offered a job starting in September at £1–10 shillings a day with a company called Fidelity Radio Ltd. I then started looking for accommodation and in those days you would not go to a letting agent but to bill boards of landlords with rooms to let in their own homes. However in those days without exception it was permissible and legal to stipulate that no dogs, blacks or Irish were welcome. This made it extremely difficult for me to find a single room and I reached a stage when I was becoming desperate as time was getting short and I feared that I would end up sleeping rough. This would have been a traumatic experience as for one I had no warm clothing and having to sleep in the open air on park benches in temperatures I was not used to could be potentially fatal.

I started my work at the factory and on the first day I was put on the production line of ten people. Our production line was responsible for producing 1000 tape recorders per week. This included assembling, testing and boxing after putting a serial number on each item and loading the products onto the same van that brought the cabinets. I was put on the beginning of the assembly line and my job was to put the speakers into the cabinet for the next person on the line to assemble the chassis until the final production. However, the cabinets which were in the cabinet manufacturer's van and had to be taken to the assembly line, all 100 of them to start production and I did not get any help from the other members of the production line who were young English lads who as far as they were concerned it was my job not theirs and no one offered any assistance because without cabinets they had nothing to do. Manual labour was not something I had experienced, as I had been a civil servant back home and lugging boxes like a 'coolie' was very degrading but I had no choice so had to persevere. The factory bell would ring at 8 am and we worked non-stop until break time at 10 am and the charge hand's responsibility was to meet the target of 100 tape recorders per day packed and loaded in the same van that brought the cabinets. If there was any slackening of the team, for example, many cabinets awaiting for the next stage of assembly at any stage of the production line the charge hand would shout, "You are up the wall, and you are holding up production." As my job entailed bolting the speakers with an electric gun, I had to be careful of the speed and timing of the screwing of the nuts and bolts which held down the speakers. Because of my nil experience of manual work I often over tightened them and split the cabinets. This resulted slowing down the production line and being threatened with the sack. This was quite a challenge but because I knew what my ambition was I persevered and learnt fast and soon gained experience and skill. The other challenges I had to overcome was to ensure that I clocked in at precisely five minutes to eight as there was a financial penalty if one was late. The working conditions left a lot to be desired as it was cold and damp located underneath the arches of the railway line and also one had to stand all day except at break times i.e. 10 minutes for tea breaks and 40 minutes for lunch. At the end of the day, I was exhausted but my day had not ended as I still had to hunt for accommodation. Autumn was coming and the days were getting cooler so this put some urgency on finding somewhere to live. The foreman soon realised that I had some intelligence and was put up the production line soldering the chassis onto the speaker leads. This meant that I no longer had to lug the cabinets from the van and this encouraged me as I was one step further up the ladder to my goal. I finally moved up the production line to testing the finished product before putting a serial number on the tape recorders ready for boxing and dispatching. I noticed one or two unusual practices at the end of this production line and I later found out the meaning of the expression 'falling off the back of the lorry'.

Occasionally the boxed finished product would be dispatched to the lorry minus a serial number which meant it did not exist and it was not counted as coming off the line even though it was in perfect working order. These 'non-existent' products ended up for sale in the Sunday markets of East London. I remembered stall holders boldly advertising some of the products they were selling were stolen and often wondered if some of them were Fidelity products.

My first wage packet was about £5 for the week as compared to my first pay packet in Trinidad which was TT$80 per month which when converted at the rate of TI$4.8/£, worked out at £4 per week. This gave me confidence that perhaps the streets of England were paved in gold held some truth as my salary had risen by £1 even as a factory worker.

Occasionally we were awarded a bonus if we hit the target for the week and this boosted my weekly income and the first thing I did was to open a post office account. My aim was to save at least £5 a month for the next two years so that I could have sufficient funds for my full-time education. Initially this was not possible but because I was sleeping on a friend's sofa for free I was able to hit my target. However, after three weeks I managed to secure a single room for the sum of £1–10 shillings/week. Needless to say I had the barest of facilities, no heating, no hot water and only had access to a cooker shared by the other residents located in a shared bathroom on the same floor. The property belonged to a Polish immigrant and needed a lot of work to be done on all floors. The basement was occupied by his elderly father and from what I knew he was living in squalor. The landlord lived on the top floor with his wife and two children and the property was clad in scaffolding most of the time. By that time in September, I had enrolled to continue my A level studies which I did four evenings per week after my 8 am to 5 pm laborious job at the factory. I coped fairly well with this work and study but by November when the evenings became colder it became quite a challenge. Even though I ate well, very often when I arrived back in my cold and damp room tired I was almost at breaking point.

Looking back I would console myself by the good progress I had made in only three months. I had a comparatively well paid job, somewhere to live, had made a few friends and started my study towards my ambition. The real test came in December when it became really cold and the temperature in my room compared with the tropics was unimaginable! The landlord just gave me an electric fire screwed to the wall at ceiling height and it did not have much effect. The other problem I had to face were the conditions in the workplace underneath the railway arch which was cold and damp and I standing on a concrete floor. To this day I cannot imagine how I survived. Like the carrot in front of a donkey I kept reaching out for it and also my pride in not admitting defeat and my unqualified ambition I must presume that kept me going. The acid test was when it snowed for the first time in January and this was the first experience of seeing snow and enduring temperatures of below freezing point. Not knowing what it was like walking on snow I had my first fall when I went out to empty the rubbish into the bin on Sunday and sustained some painful bruises, my only consolation was being able to snuggle up under the blankets and sleeping until 7 am the next morning in time to force myself to go to work, as if you miss a day's work you not only loose a day's wage you also miss out on the potential weekly bonus. The working conditions and the harsh contractual rules were made to ensure that the workers gave their 'pound of flesh' to the company. I also chose to walk to work to save money and coming from the tropics I did not have sturdy shoes or adequate clothing.

The foreman recognised my ability to learn quickly, and he recommended that I should be moved to a more technical job and I was subsequently moved to the section which did the alignment of the transistor radios called the 'Coronet' one of the products the factory produced. I was really getting somewhere now; firstly the room was warm and I was given a chair and I was no longer on the production line as such. My job was to tune the radio to pick up Radio Luxembourg and Radio Caroline stations as well as the British radio stations. I enjoyed working in this department and was often offered overtime work on Saturdays and this boosted my weekly pay and I started hitting my £5 target for savings. My social life was very limited because even going to the cinema was expensive. However, because I liked a bit of dancing I used to go to the Hammersmith Pallais hoping to meet a member of the opposite sex. Luckily no such thing happened as it would have caused me to be distracted from my main goal. I worked at this factory for two years without a holiday and managed to save a significant amount towards maintaining me during full time education. One of the friends I met on the S.S. Southern Cross I met by chance in the Shepard's

Bush market. After telling him how uncomfortable the room I was living in was, he invited me to join him in his basement flat where he had a spare room. I immediately accepted his invitation but as required I had to give one week's notice to the landlord, come what may, then subsequently moved to his flat in Shepherd's Bush which was not too far away from Latimer Road Tube Station. The accommodation was far superior to what I had and the flat was well heated with kerosene heaters but no hot water. Also I joined his family for meals so I had three square meals over the weekends and a home cooked dinner during the week. I was in seventh heaven! I continued to work with Fidelity Radio and in those two years I had one month's holiday to Europe with my older wealthy cousin from Trinidad who was on a three month vacation in the UK. By the end of the second year, I had obtained the necessary qualifications to start a degree course at the North London University. To achieve this I had to work during the day do part time study at night and spend most of my Saturdays in the local library in the reading section on the second floor and as a bonus it was centrally heated. There were many other immigrant students using the facilities this met with some opposition from the local community because they often complained that the place was taken over by immigrants. I eventually sacked from my post in the factory in August 1963 because I refused to comply with one of the requests by the owner of the factory. The reason for this was that there were regular break-ins at weekends and at the last break in foot prints were left on the roof connected to the archway. He suspected that it must be an 'inside job' and he went to all the production lines and demanded to see the soles of the workers' shoes for any signs of paint that corresponded to the paint on the roof. I refused on the grounds that it was done inappropriately and in an embarrassing manner which reminded me of how immigrants were treated by their employers in the UK and somewhat similar to the treatment handed out by the English foremen to the indentured labourers in Trinidad who had no rights. By this time, I had sufficient funds to continue my studies full time. There were only two weeks before my university course started. I rejected his demand when he tapped me on the back and demanded in an aggressive way that I lift my left foot up and then my right to examine my shoes. I rejected his demand and was sacked on the spot and asked to leave immediately with no redundancy payment but I was given my last week's pay and my P45. I was now a free agent full of confidence and looking forward to the next stage of gaining my qualifications at university in September.

Chapter 6
Paying My Way
Through University

September 1963 was a significant date towards my goal of becoming a chartered electronic engineer. By now, I had been accepted by the North London University to start my course in radio and electronic engineering and by that time I had saved enough funds to see me through the first year as was the situation at that time students had to find their own accommodation, and I obtained the cheapest single room I could find.

Again there was difficulty finding this because the situation at the time was that most English landlords would not accept immigrants. I eventually found a single room with a Greek Cypriot family on the ground floor and had to share the bathroom and other facilities with the family. There was no hot water or washing facilities in the room but the only consolation was that it was in walking distance of the college. As I had limited use of the kitchen, my breakfast was basic cornflakes and lunch and tea which I had in the restaurant at the college. The weekends were not too bad because to supplement my fees and living costs I took a part- time job working in a restaurant in Leicester Square from 3 pm to 11 pm so I had most of my meals at reduced price at the restaurant; however, the work was very demanding washing dishes together with two other immigrants till 11 pm. The pay was not anything to write home about but it suited me as I had somewhere warm to work but back at my accommodation there was no heating. Also it was rather damp and worsening as the year progressed towards winter.

The money I earned part time helped to subsidise my rent and weekly groceries also a little to put away for my second year at university. The landlord was not very friendly, and there were many restrictions like no radio noise and being in by 8 pm and no use of the bath. I did shower myself regularly at the college gymnasium as I joined the cricket club when we had indoor practice most evenings. I had a bit of a setback financially when one evening my wallet was stolen when I hung up my clothes whilst I had a shower. This situation was tolerable until the dampness of my rented room became so uncomfortable that I decided to find alternative accommodation. Tramping the streets after dark at the end of lectures was not very safe but by then it was difficult to see the adverts of rental accommodation on the bill board of the corner shop. I was at the end of my tether and was at the point of jacking it all in and make arrangements to return to Trinidad; however, there was someone above guarding me and out of the blue I had a vision to visit the British Council in Portland Street opposite the BBC broadcasting headquarters. I was directed to the accommodation officer who was dealing with accommodation for immigrants who were recruited by the British Council to work as nurses, bus drivers and labourers etc. I described my situation with the administrator. I did not come under that category, but he said I could try the Alliance Club in Bedford's Square, a Christian Association which helps overseas students to find accommodation. After being given the address, I set off to try my luck.

I was very disappointed when I was told there were no vacancies nor would there be any in the foreseeable future but the warden said to me that there was another Alliance Club being set up that week in Newington Green. This was good news to me as it was in walking distance from the university. So I said a little prayer and immediately headed to the address of the hostel. Approaching the building I saw that it was called The China Inland Mission which made me think that I was at the wrong address. However, I went through the impressive archway and knocked on the door only to be greeted by an elderly person who I later found out that he was the head of the CIM He informed me that these were offices and lecture halls only as the number of missionaries to China had diminished and the residences at the rear of the offices were for missionaries on training. He directed me to the hall of residence. I was greeted by the warden Mr Hillson-Smith with a very welcoming broad smile informing me that I was in the right place:

The Evangelical Christian Alliance Club Hostel for overseas students, and he told me that I was the very first student to be welcomed into the hall of residence. It was warm centrally heated, and after showing me to the room that was available I immediately accepted the offer to stay there at £5.00/week with all meals included. I booked in to start the following Monday even though I knew I had to give my landlord a week's notice. It was a Wednesday that I informed him that I was leaving on Monday and was informed that I had to pay a week's rent in advance or give a week's notice. The dampness in my room was unbearable and after my weekend job I arrived home on Sunday and made the decision to leave with or without the landlord's agreement. I refused to pay the rent for the following week and I was unable to get into my room after college on the Monday as the landlord had locked me out. I went to the police station and explained my situation and they were very sympathetic and he sent a police officer with me to speak to the landlord. He was very afraid and became very compliant and opened the building for me to collect my possessions after the police officer had left. The landlord insisted that I remove my possessions immediately by putting them out on the pavement not allowing me time to arrange transport to my new accommodation. I had to go to the main road to get a taxi but on return to where my belongings were I found that most of it had been stolen.

My suit case with my clothing was still there; however, this was convenient because the other things that I had accumulated would not be needed in my new home.

I arrived at my new accommodation at 6 pm and by that time other students were already in residence. I was taken to my room to settle in before the evening meal that was being served at 7 pm. I thought I had gone to heaven with a room that was centrally heated, a wash basin with hot and cold water and a bed with crisp white sheets and a newly decorated room with a polished floor.

Most of the intake of new residents were students from overseas but the meal was a traditional English three course dinner of soup followed by meat, potatoes and two vegetables meal and a pudding of peaches and cream. We all sat on the same long table and there were students from South America, Rhodesia, Singapore, Fiji, New Zealand, India, Kenya and a few English students also a couple of West Indians including myself. I soon made friends because we all spoke English, although with different accents, we all understood each other. After dinner, we were directed to the common room where coffee was being served. All this was so different to what I had endured for the last two years that I began to have visions of Eldorado the city of gold!

The warden explained to us that it was a Christian organisation and there would be a Bible study in the common room every evening but this was not compulsory for students to attend. He said we could have as many baths as we wanted which was music to my ears and also there were facilities such as a snooker table and table tennis tables in the basement and a tennis court in the grounds which could all be used by the residents free of charge. I was now truly on my way towards my goal. There was after all some truth in that the pavements of London are paved with gold but one had to search hard to find it!

Chapter 7
Coping with University Life

By now, I was as happy as a sand boy with my accommodation and after the first term I was convinced that I had chosen the right course and the experience I had gained fending for myself and also the time working in a factory was paying off. My bank balance was gradually heading towards red and I had to supplement my living cost by part time work. I was offered an evening job to look after the boilers in the basement of the hostel which involved stoking the boilers. This work was very demanding and I often ending up with singed eyebrows when opening the boiler to feed it with coke. Also I was given a weekend job at the hostel doing the washing up. These incomes supplemented my living fees and I even had some excess to purchase my first bicycle second hand for £5 and also a guitar. Unfortunately the bicycle was stolen within the first week and my ambition to learn to play the guitar was short lived as I am tone deaf!

I made many friends including a number of English students, and I joined them attending a local church near the hostel and up to today I am still in touch with them and will write later about them because they played a very significant part in my future life. My first Christmas was quite an experience because first of all we had invites from local churches to socialise and I had many friends with whom to enjoy the celebrations.

During the Christmas break I found full-time employment with the post office delivering Christmas mail and was an assistant to a regular postman; a very pleasant person but he invariably allocated me to areas where there were many high rise blocks of flats and chose streets of normal houses to deliver mail for himself. The lifts often didn't work which meant that I had to climb many stairs to deliver letters. This income boosted my bank balance and I was becoming more confident that I would have sufficient funds for my second year at university. My daily living expenses were minimal as I had two sumptuous meals per day included in the rent at the hostel and lunch at the college was just a cheese roll and a cup of tea.

I completed my first year successfully and since I had sufficient funds for the second year I decided to see a bit of England by way of hitch hiking. I reserved my accommodation until September, joined the youth hostel association, bought a ruck sack and a sleeping bag and set off early for my hitch hiking adventure. My intention was to get as far north as possible and hitch hike from east to west from Hartlepool through Cumbria to Workington on the west coast. This was the intention as I had worked out on the youth hostel map where the various youth hostels were but I did not achieve the goal which will become apparent later in my memoirs.

I found myself on the A 40 the road to Oxford and to my surprise after giving usual thumbs up hitch hiking sign I was lucky enough to be offered a lift by a lorry driver someone going to Oxford and we were able to exchange information about ourselves and when I stated that I was from Trinidad he explained to me how he enjoyed going to the Caribbean on holidays. He dropped me off in the centre of Oxford and I was able to find my way to my first youth hostel which proved to be quite an experience. The warden welcomed me and after showing him my membership card he offered me a room where there were 12 of us sharing a dormitory of bunk beds. He explained to me the rules of the hostel including the chores I was to be allocated and the rules of the bedroom and the self-catering kitchen but above all the behaviour in the common room where most of the people were students from various parts of the world. I managed to prepare myself a meal from a tin but this was not easy because the kitchen was used by many groups but eventually I managed to get a slot to use the stove. The first night was quite an experience because the common room in the evening was filled with students chattering but I managed to make a few friends but the surprise was the bedroom which was filled with the indescribable smells of socks and body odours! The bed had only a blanket and a pillow but it was comfortable enough with my cotton sleeping bag and being summer it was sufficient to get a good night's sleep. I also managed to limit myself to the £1 per day as my budget.

The next day I had my breakfast and did my chore which was sweeping all the mats and tidying the hostel entrance. I hit the road at 9.30 am Sunday morning and did the usual thumbs up sign on the nearest main road. I did not have to wait for more than half an hour when a posh looking car stopped and when I informed the person I was going to the

Lake District he invited me to join him as he was going to Dundee as a university lecturer for the week. Again we exchanged information about ourselves, my ambitions and he said that he himself was a hitch hiker during his summer vacations when a student but mainly in Europe.

It seems as though I was carrying a lucky charm with me or people thought that I looked safe enough to pick up. To my surprise the gentleman said to me that he was going to have lunch and he invited me to join him for Sunday lunch. I graciously accepted his invitation and was treated to a three course lunch including soup, roast beef and the traditional Yorkshire puddings and lashings of roast potatoes and vegetables. This was followed by apple pie and custard and washed down by coffee. Luckily he said to me that I needn't worry about the bill as he would put it on his expense account.

This was luck more than judgement and a real blessing because apart from getting to my destination I had a full stomach and no extra expenses that day because when I arrived at the hostel I did not need a meal. I had a few cream crackers in my rucksack which were sufficient to keep me going until next morning. I stayed in the Lake District for a few days, first of all at Ambleside then Keswick and finally Windermere. I met quite a few interesting people at the youth hostels one of whom was a 70-year-old cyclist. He showed me his youth hostel map and said it was his intention to visit all the youth hostels in England, Wales and Scotland and by the markings on his map he had already done quite a number! I met quite a number of students from Germany, France, Holland and Italy and they informed me that hitch hiking in Europe was quite easy and that the hostels were as comfortable and cheap as in England. This I thought would be my next adventure during the following summer.

The most interesting person I met in the Lake District was a professional photographer, and when I told him that I was hoping to get as far as Scotland but had no time scale or any definite bookings and that I was footloose and fancy free he invited me to join him but warned that he would be going mainly to the western side of Scotland in out of the way places that were nevertheless very picturesque. He told me he was prepared to take me anywhere he went but he would expect me to carry his equipment I agreed with this arrangement and for three days I stayed with him in various youth hostels and we went to some very interesting places including ancient castles, and I also saw some wonderful sunsets. These were the sort of things the photographer was aiming to capture on film. He was a good companion and I always had someone to talk to in the evenings but unfortunately he also expected me to provide him with his breakfast in the morning and in one instance to do his 'chore' because he wanted to do some early morning shoots.

It was at Ullapool that I decided to break off with him so I woke up early enough before him, packed my bags and set off on my own to continue my hitch hiking towards John o' Groats. When I reached John O'Groats, I had been traveling for about three weeks. I decided to hitch hike my way back home and even though I had had showers at the hostels my clothing was much in need of laundering. My first stop was Ullapool where I had been before and was well known by the warden and his family because of an incident involving them. His seven-year-old daughter who followed me to the beach unknown to them and after a while there was a search for her and there was much relief when we both returned about an hour later. The child explained that we were playing skimming stones onto the sea and they were satisfied that I hadn't lured her away. (Many years after wards I took my fiancée there, who is now my wife), and the warden and his wife remembered me. I then hitch hiked to Fort Williams and stayed there a couple of days after which I decided to head for Oban. I was lucky again when I was picked up by a vicar and his family even though I was soaking wet from the rain. I was taken to their home, dried out and had some home cooking before setting off towards Edinburgh. On my way there, I stayed a night in Stirling Castle and then spent a day in Edinburgh visiting the sights and the castle.

I headed homewards via the Lake District and thence to Oxford and finally back to the Alliance Club. In all, I had been away for 8 weeks.

I started my second year at university, and as I had done in the first year I had to do some part time work some in a West End restaurant and also at Christmas time I did mail delivery again. In addition to this, I did casual work at the hostel washing dishes but decided not to do boiler stoking again! My studies were going well and I was heading for a successful third year.

Chapter 8
Qualified as an Electronic Engineer

During my final year at university I went for a number of interviews, as it was done at the time in the second term of the final year, with several companies including the BBC, British Telecom EMI, GEC, and Marconi. I was offered a job with EMI in Hayes Middlesex and was awaiting the results of my other interviews and these offers were conditional on my passing my final examinations. I qualified in May 1966 as an electronic and radio engineer and also became a graduate member of the Institution of Electronic and Radio Engineers. I was then offered a post in the research department of EMI television section as a junior electronic engineer. However I kept my options open in case I got a better offer in London by the BBC or British Telecommunications.

On the 1st of June, I started my job with EMI 1966 and by then my bank balance was almost in the red. The office was in Middlesex and I was in North London and I had sufficient money to pay for my fares on the first day. I remember fully well having an interview with the personnel officer on the first day and explaining my predicament of not being able to pay my fare home on that day. I explained that

I had supported myself through university by saving and working part time and that my bank balance was in the red. I was given a loan of £100 from their petty cash and it was the start of my way to Eldorado.

I received my first salary and my life began changing from a poor student to becoming a well-to-do bachelor. My first objective was to clothe myself properly as a professional with a Burton suit and all the trappings of a successful person. My attitude to life had changed dramatically over night, I began making friends, going to the cinema, and I looked forward to the weekends because I was able to afford to join my friends to parties and dance halls. I was now also able to afford a single room at the hostel as I was allowed to continue living there even though I was no longer a student. I made many new close friends from the UK in that place and up to today I am still in contact with them. I will expand on that later on. I socialised with my English friends frequently, we went to the same church, learnt to ice skate at Queen's ice rink in Streatham and went ten pin bowling in Queensway. By then, I had started looking for a soul mate because for the past five years I could not contemplate getting involved with the opposite sex mainly because of limited finance and needing to concentrate on my studies. My other ambition was to learn to drive and purchase an E Type Jag which was about £1500 at the time, one and a half times my annual wage! I started saving towards this and at one stage I could see where I could have achieved the ambition of having a smart car and also of putting down a deposit on a house in the next 5 years.

Unfortunately my mother who lived in Trinidad passed away and I had to break into my savings to finance my fares home.

Sadly my father had passed away whilst I was at university during my final exams and I was advised by my family that it would be better to finish my finals than to go home for his funeral.

However, I continued enjoying my success, and I could see that London's pavements were paved with gold if one looked for it, worked hard and had ambition. A number of my compatriots, who I sailed within 1961 to England, returned to the mother land, possibly they were not as successful as I was in seeking their fortunes and improving their lives as they fell by the wayside, possibly because of family commitments, or got distracted in other directions.

Chapter 9
Travel and Falling in Love

I was now ready for enjoying the fruits of my labour and I started going to the cinemas and theatres and socialising with my friends. I was invited to join a group of friends, three men and four girls to a camping holiday to Italy. We hired a Dorm mobile camper van and the necessary camping equipment and set off for Italy. We took the ferry from Dover to Calais, drove across France, Switzerland and then through the St Bernard's pass to Italy. The girls were all nurses, slept in the Dorm mobile and us men set up our tents. We budgeted so that we would cook our own meals in the camp sites and all the chores were equally divided. On a few occasions, the alpha female who controlled the budget arranged for us to have a meal in a restaurant. We visited Florence, Milan, and got as far as Venice where we stayed for a few days.

We then worked our way southwards to Rome where we enjoyed all the famous sights and then made our way to Naples where we were fascinated by the narrow streets with peoples' washing strung across the street between the houses. It was noticed that certain people were pairing up but even though I had my eye on one of the girls I was not one of the lucky ones. Overall the tour went well and the friendship between us all grew stronger.

When we returned to London, we continued to go out together, ice skating and tenpin bowling. The following year a trip was organised to go to North Africa but this time the boys decided to buy a camper van and as one of the boys was a mechanic he brought it up to roadworthy standard. This time there were more of us, six boys and three girls. In August 1968, we set off to France by the Dover ferry, drove through France and into Spain camping along the way. The campsites were well chosen as they were recommended by the AA and they all had good facilities and sometimes in France they had English style toilets instead of the French type! We travelled down the Spanish coast via Benidorm and Torremolinos which were not built up as they are today. On the Southern tip of Spain, we took a ferry from Algeciras to Ceuta in Morocco. We visited Tangiers, Rabat and Casablanca and we found that all of the camp sites were very high standard, secure and even had security guards. In one of the local souks, we did some bargaining for some leather goods and for a bit of jest and leg pulling one of the girls was offered in exchange but the Moroccan merchant refused saying that she was too skinny and Moroccans like their women with a bit of flesh!

Nevertheless we purchased hand bags, pouffes and other leather items after battering for a good price stating at half the price they asked for until we came to an agreement of around 25% of the asking price. This is the traditional way of buying things in the souks including fruit, vegetables and meat. We consumed a fair bit of beef as it was a reasonable price compared to English prices. It wasn't long before we realised that we hadn't seen any cows and later discovered that camel's meat was called beef. As there were many flies on the meat, we cooked it very well and it was quite tasty.

We continued on and stayed at a camp site near Marrakesh where we went looking for the advertised swimming pool to have a swim as the temperature was getting unbearable but when we found the site the pool was empty because of drought conditions. We retreated back to the shade of our tent and the van as the shade it was 120 degrees F! Unfortunately, two of our friends suffered heat stroke and we had to go into town to buy salt tablets to make salty orangeade as a cure. I had my legs pulled as they said, "It's all right for you, Harry, as you are fully baked but we were taken out of the oven early!"

We continued towards the edge of the Sahara but because of the high temperature and the fact that the van was designed for temperate conditions it kept overheating after only short distances. There was a risk in that the van would break down completely and even though we had AA membership after about 100 miles south of Marrakesh we decided to turn back for home. Since we liked the site in Marrakesh we thought we would go back to that site and see a bit of night life there, in particular the snake charmers and story tellers in the main square.

After supper, the group decided to go into town but they asked for volunteer to look after the tent and the van. I volunteered with one of the girls to stay behind. By now, people were really pairing up and I had my eyes on one particular girl for some time and it seems that the girl who also had a good reason for wanting to stay behind too to look after the van. It was a warm night and under a black velvet sky studded with diamonds we lay on a blanket and gazed heavenward. We talked and talked and realised that we had so much in common and were on the same page. At that point I fell madly in love. After that, we were inseparable and the others started noticing, seeing us holding hands and sitting next to each other. There was a bit of jealousy from a couple of the other guys but by that time the alpha male and alpha female had already paired off. They were the ones who organised the trip and controlled the purse even down to purchasing ice- creams and other Moroccan delights. We then headed back to Ceuta and some days drove more than a 100 miles a day as the driving was shared by three other people and the roads were in very good condition.

We got back to Spain and travelled towards Bilbao to catch a ferry to Southampton. On the ferry, we realised we were really in love because at one stage we got separated for almost an hour and became frantic to get back together. When we arrived at Southampton, we went to the alpha male parents' hotel in Bournemouth where we stayed for the weekend. I got to know my girlfriend a bit more and to express my love for her I gave her my signet ring which she joyously accepted which indicated that we were an item. On the way back to London, we were invited for lunch at my girlfriend's parent's house in New Malden in Surrey. I was introduced to them as a friend only but I rather thought that her mother was suspicious that there was something between us.

Before we parted, we arranged our first date to meet the following Sunday at All Soul's Church in Langham Place near the BBC broadcasting headquarters not far from the British Council were in my opinion was turning point in my road to success and the start of gathering the nuggets of gold from the pavements of London. Our planned meeting was at Oxford Circus Station at 10.30 am for the start of the service at 11 am. At about 10.45, there was a knock on my door informing me that there was a phone call for me. When I answered it, I heard the question, "Where are you?" and then I realised I had forgotten our date and the thought came to my mind that I had blown it irrevocably. However, I apologised and found my way to the station and she was gracious enough to accept that I had over slept. We were crept into the service which was more than half way through but we were able to go up into the gallery where there were not many people without too much disturbance. We had arrived in time for the sermon from the preacher John Stott a well- known evangelist who attracted many university students. We met quite a few people during the coffee time after the service and a couple of them who were resident at the Alliance Club later played a significant part in our life.

During the following few months we regularly met to walk along the Embankment went to many shows in the West End and it was convenient for us to meet at Waterloo Station as my girlfriend had moved to Kingston Hospital to do her midwifery training. Unfortunately, I could not entertain her in the Alliance Club as there were certain restrictions on female visitors neither could we meet at her home because there was parental opposition to our relationship.

Consequently we spent many hours walking up and down the Embankment in the cold ending up at the Royal Festival Hall cafe to warm up with a cup of coffee. We went to concerts there and saw many famous people like Ray Charles and other popular musicians. One of the highlights was dinner at the Festival Hall followed by seeing the ballet Swan Lake. These events had to be booked well in advance and because of my disposable income I was able to afford the cost of the tickets. We also went to the proms at the Albert Hall for which you just had to queue for standing places("in the gods"). However, this was somewhere to go and also convenient for us to maximise our evenings together and having a last kiss before the last train to my girlfriend's home and also the last bus number 73 to Newington Green North London. It was amazing what love drives you to do and on at least two occasions I missed the last bus and had to walk to my home from Waterloo station to the Alliance Club. At one point, I was invited to join our group of friends to a Christian convention in Keswick and it was the night before I had missed both the tube and the bus and spent most of the night walking home and I had about one hour's sleep before being picked up to go to the Lake District.

Needless to say I slept all the way there not letting the others know why I was so tired and sleepy. Sadly my girlfriend was unable to join me as she was working at the hospital where she was doing midwifery training.

Our relationship blossomed and I was invited to the Christmas Ball at Kingston Hospital which was very romantic and this made our relationship even closer. That Christmas was invited to spend the holiday with my German friend's family in Baden in South Germany. I had a great time experiencing the German customs at Christmas but when I returned to the UK. I went down with the flu due to me getting chilled at Frankfurt Station where I had agreed to meet up with another friend from Singapore who was spending Christmas with his German girlfriend's family with whom I was going to spend a few days before returning to London.

Unfortunately we got our am and pm mixed up. I thought he meant 7 am but his idea was 7 pm which meant that I waited for a long time checking train after train without seeing him. At 6.30 pm, I caught the last train to Calais and then to London. I was quite ill and had two weeks off work and it was very distressing for us both as we were unable to meet up. Finally after I had recovered I made a booking at the restaurant at the top of the post office tower, the tallest building in London at the time. The revolving restaurant was open to the public then but was later permanently closed due to the threat of IRA bombings. There was also a fantastic viewing platform and I thought it was the ideal place to propose as it seemed as though it was a continuation of our Marrakesh experience under the starry sky.

After a delicious dinner, I took my girlfriend to the viewing platform and I asked her to marry me to which she said yes! I did not have a ring to put on her finger but the next day we went to Oxford Street together and chose an engagement ring and the knot was irrevocably sealed by putting the ring on her finger as is the custom. It was the 25th of January 1969.

We continued going to the theatre and cinema and had romantic meetings on the embankment finishing by going to the Festival Hall for a coffee to warm up. My next ambition was to purchase a car but first I had to pass my driving test which I eventually passed after the 4th attempt. This was due to the company sending me on a two weeks' driving course as my job involved driving to Cornwall and taking equipment with me. My first car was an Austin A 30 with four doors which I purchased with my Tasmanian Friend which cost us the princely sum of £40 which included four new tyres and a battery. It eventually became my property when my Tasmanian friend returned to his homeland. As a matter of interest, he caught up with me many years later and he reminded me that he still had the key to the Austin DEH901. He got my e-mail after reading an article I wrote on reviewing one of the cruises that I had been on with my wife. I was in my element now having graduated, getting a well-paid job, purchasing a car and being engaged. My next plan was to start saving up to purchase a house before setting a date for our marriage. My fiancé and myself started looking for a house on the cheaper side of London and as I was working at BT headquarters near Liverpool Street Station. We started looking in Hornchurch where my friend who was later to be my best man lived. We eventually thought that we had found the right property within our budget but after getting the result of the survey we were informed that the property needed underpinning and we were advised not to go ahead with the deal as the cost would be exorbitant. We were devastated and somewhat depressed but after 24 hours of despair our friend said he had been made redundant and they were putting up their house for sale and he offered the property to us which we gladly accepted. We had another stroke of luck as my fiancé inherited some money from a great aunt and together with three times my salary and half of her salary we were able to put down the required deposit for the house. The great advantage of this was that we did not need a survey and a reduction was made in consideration of saving estate agent's fees. The price of the property was £5,500 and the remainder to be paid over 25 years at £36 per month, which was a third of my monthly income. We were now in a position to set a date for our marriage and has we had no one to consult on the date we literally sat in our car outside Waterloo Station near where earlier the previous year we made that momentous decision to stay together. We casually stuck a pin in the 1970 calendar and came up with the 11th of April. The next day we instructed our solicitor to start negotiations to purchase this property in which we live to this day.

We set about arranging our marriage and since we lived in different parishes we had to have the banns read both in Islington and Westminster as my fiancé had moved back to working at Westminster Hospital after completing her midwifery training. Our ceremony was to be held in St Stephen's Church Highbury and my best man was the person from whom we bought the house and as he was a longstanding friend. The warden of the Alliance Club agreed to escort my wife to be to the altar due to the continued opposition from her parents to our marriage. The Club agreed to cater for the reception. We also booked our honeymoon in Guernsey at the Fermain Bay Hotel and the scene was now set. The cost of the reception was £30 and the honeymoon including the flight and all meal was about £35. All the residents at the club were invited and quite a few of my wife's relatives attended including her aunts and her grandmother and I was fortunate to have my sister there as well.

On the 11th April, a limousine was sent to the home of my wife's paternal grandparents where she was staying prior to the wedding as surprisingly they had accepted our relationship even though they were from the older generation. The ceremony went according to plan and we even had a friend from the club who agreed to play the organ free of charge and the church choir also did the honours. On a sad note, one of the girls in the choir was killed in the Moorgate train crash that year.

The reception went smoothly and a good friend took us to the airport to fly to Guernsey for our honeymoon. We even had our wedding photo in the local newspaper and this was brought to my attention by one of the cleaners in my office in London. The honeymoon was great and we were on cloud nine! I was now starting to look back on the progress I had made from the day in 1961 when I arrived in Southampton. The purchase of the house was making good progress and we were in a very unusual situation as when we returned from Guernsey we lived with our best man and his wife until the contracts were finalised. They had difficulty finalising their own contract to where they were moving.

However, this worked out to both of our benefits and this situation was not made known to our respective solicitors.

Chapter 10
Ups and Downs in the First Two Years of Marriage

On the 1st of June 1970, our friends moved out of the house which was now ours and we helped them to move into their home where he was going to be a sub-postmaster in the village shop in Wraysbury, Berkshire. Our new home was a three bedroomed semi-detached property and we started our life there with only a mattress and a cooker as our friends took their furniture with them. The first thing we bought was a card table and two stools. My wife's travel trunk with a blanket throw was our first settee. We lived like this until furniture that we had ordered from the local department store arrived. For a whole year, we did not venture out anywhere because it was so lovely to have our own place and we had seen so many shows and concerts and spent hours in the cold on the Thames Embankment that we were just happy to sit in front of the Raeburn coal fire with each other for company. We started decorating the rooms to our taste and we had a number of mishaps as we had no experience of DIV. The first one was wallpapering an entire room with ready pasted paper and although we followed the instructions the following morning the paper was not on the walls but on the floor! The other mishap was stripping the old wallpaper with a steamer and because of our lack of experience we left the steamer on the wall longer than necessary steam had penetrated the cracks in the plaster causing it to crumble and fall off. However, we learnt as we went and have since developed skills not only wallpapering but plumbing and electrical installation which was legal to do at that time. We had parked our car with some difficulty into the garage via the awkward shaped drive. After a while, we decided to have a drive around and on reversing the car into the drive the bumper got stuck on the gate post and it was then we got to know our neighbour next door who came to our rescue who had to saw the gatepost off to release the car. We developed a deep friendship with them after that incident and they were good neighbours ever since. They realised that we were lacking in furniture and they offered us their settee which they were going to replace. On discovering that we were expecting our first baby, they offered us their son's old cot and highchair and other items. We also found a church which we joined and have attended there ever since.

Our first daughter was born shortly after our first anniversary on the 21st of April 1971. And we enjoyed parenthood and started making friends from the church and also continued the relationship with the friends with whom we had holidayed with before our marriage. 50 years later we still meet up as a group every six months and have fellowship together. During that year I continued working in the satellite department at BT headquarters in London and the work involved development of satellite communication BT Tell Star and the tracking station was located in Cornwall.

I spent many days away from home and on occasion my wife and small daughter joined me and we stayed in a bed and breakfast in a little village called Porthallow on the coast. I gained a considerable amount of experience on this new technology and together with the various training I had had in the training centre at Staffordshire I was hoping for early promotion. During this time I had visions of returning to my homeland and had many thoughts and anxious moments about this desire. At this point, it would be a very difficult decision as I now had a home, a wife and a baby daughter and an enjoyable job.

I kept my ear to the ground and out of the blue I saw an advertisement in the Daily Telegraph of an advertisement by the Trinidad Government for an experienced Trinidad national in satellite communication. The Government of that country as it was now an independent state within the Commonwealth had taken over 51% of the ownership of the space telecommunication department of Cable and Wireless Ltd. The post was for a manager designate of the tracking station in Matura on the East coast of the island. I was very excited and started to think seriously of applying for this post but I was in this great dilemma of the unknown consequences of resigning from a well-paid job and disrupting a stable home situation. I had many sleepless nights and kept my desire to myself for some time and started weighing the pros and cons of any decisions. I eventually mentioned the advertised job to my wife and we had a long discussion about it and my wife was not particularly dismayed and did not show any anxiety about leaving her homeland even though she was an only child had we had a home and was very happy with our situation.

We finally made that decision and I put in an application to the Trinidad Government. I was invited to take up a post as the manager designate of the tracking station. I did not want to burn my bridges and wanted to play safe and I went to my departmental head and applied for special leave 'C' and I was given six months without pay and my position was secured for that period and I had the right to return to my post. I did not let out when I accepted my new post that it was only for six months in order not to jeopardise any negotiation in connection with salary and concessions. The scene was now set for us to make arrangements to travel to the West Indies by ship and unlike when I came to England 2nd class we were to go 1st class paid for by the Trinidad and Tobago government. This was a useful mode of transport as we could take most of our furniture on board.

As I wanted to keep our options open, we decided to put our house in the hands of an estate agent to let it out unfurnished for one year. We then had some problems because instead of sailing from Southampton we had to fly to Amsterdam and get on a Dutch boat which was scheduled to sail to the Dutch West Indies and as such our cargo went on a different ship. The day came for us to leave and it was thick fog on the morning of the 1st of December 1971. Luckily the fog lifted the next day and we were able to fly to Holland to catch the boat from Rotterdam which was to sail the following day. We were booked in a hotel in Rotterdam for the night before but unfortunately I came down with influenza and was delirious with a high fever. My wife kept her head and on the morning of our departure she called a taxi and bundled me 12 pieces of luggage and our eight- month-old baby into the taxi and instructed the driver to take us to the docks. She pushed everything up the gangplank including me and we were checked into our cabin where I stayed for the next three days feeling rather ill. It turned out that many people on the ship caught my flu via the air conditioning but somehow my wife Margaret and baby daughter Sara did not get infected.

I was very comfortable in first class compared with my experience on the Southern Cross when I was put to dine with the first class passengers, who were mainly Australians, in 1961. In the previous ten years, I had changed from an inexperienced village boy to a mature executive engineer with lots of experience of business life. Crossing the North Atlantic in December the sea was rather rough and choppy. The ship was designed to pitch but not roll so sea sickness was kept to a minimum and we were at sea for ten days before we saw land in the form of San Martin our first port of call. In the Caribbean, the sea was now calm and the temperature was now high enough to swim in the swimming pool however we did not know it was a cargo ship and as the swimming pool was above the cargo hold it had to be drained to open the hold and was no longer available as we sailed on via other Dutch islands such as Curacao and Aruba to discharge cargo and reload with the produce of those islands. When we got near to the harbour of Port of Spain, the ship anchored and a tender came from shore to collect us to take us to the port. It was déjà vu for me as that was where I was a custom officer together with my brother who was still working there as one of the senior custom officers. We had VIP treatment as we did not have to queue up at immigration or have customs checks on our luggage as my brother came to meet us on the tender and he took care of all the formalities.

Later we drove to his home as we had not yet made arrangements of having our own accommodation. The first night was a bit of an experience for my wife because of the heat, the constant barking of dogs, mooing of the cow next door and sleeping under a mosquito net. However, even I was a bit taken aback but memories soon came back that, that was as it was before I left ten years previously in 1961. We arrived one week before Christmas on 18th of December 1971 and I then started counting the nuggets of gold I had gathered from the streets of London, my qualification as an electronic engineer, a beautiful wife, a darling daughter, and a senior management job at the tracking station.

My brother and his family were very welcoming and my wife was able to fall into the different culture with ease and soon got the hang of the accent and even I started losing my so called 'Oxford' accent which I had acquired in England. My wife got on well with my brother's three daughters and her sister-in-law, even Sara got used to the heat very quickly. The climate was like the hottest days of an English summer but very humid and she soon became acclimatised. On Christmas morning, we rose at 3 am to get ready in time for the 5 am service at the local Presbyterian Church which was established by the Canadian missionaries. After the service, we visited various relatives for drinks and snacks and returned home before it became too hot. This tradition was of course not new to me but it was so different to what I had experienced in England for the last ten years. There was a traditional luncheon feast of various curried meats, dhal puree which is like a chapatti filled with dhal and various sweet meats instead of Christmas pudding. Later in the day when it started getting cooler people started visiting each other and ended up at the person who had the largest house where there was singing and dancing and continuation of the celebration of the birth of Jesus Christ. So began our new life in Trinidad which we hoped would be for some time but didn't know at this point how things would turn out.

Chapter 11
Shattered Dreams in My Homeland

I was given two weeks to settle into my new environment and also an opportunity to find suitable accommodation. It was important to find accommodation as soon as possible as we were living in cramped conditions at my brother's house. This proved to be quite an ordeal because unlike England there were no estate agents or agencies advertising houses for rent and we depended on the recommendation from friends and relatives. The places we viewed were way below the standard that I expected to start my new life and it was the first disappointment I had to face. My dream of my enhancement in this area was shattered and this caused me to think again as to whether I had made the right decision and even made me contemplate returning back to the UK where we had our own three bed room semi-detached property. However, we had a stroke of luck and we were offered alternative accommodation with my cousin whose daughter had just started further education in Canada and there was a spare room in his home which we gladly accepted.

I was posted at the tracking station which was one hour away from headquarters and transportation was provided for me and the other technicians working at the tracking station.

I was conveniently housed near to the pickup point and was picked up at 7 am every morning. After the first week, I learnt that the expatriate technicians were living in luxury and provided with a house, domestic help and even a gardener; they were also provided with a car for their personal use. I approached higher management and informed them of the predicament I had in finding suitable affordable accommodation and requested that as a manager I should be given the same perks as the Cable and Wireless expatriate technicians. I was disappointed when I was informed they were not prepared to meet my demand as they would also have to provide the same conditions for the other local technicians. I was infuriated at this treatment as it was 11 years since I had left Trinidad and I needed some assistance in resettling. I then went to the General Manager of 'Textel', the company who were in partnership with Cable and Wireless, and was offered the derisory sum of $100 TT (the equivalent of £20 Sterling) and a loan was offered to purchase a car but not as a perk. I continued looking for accommodation and shadowed the existing manager from whom I was to take over the running of the tracking station. We became friendly with him and the other English expatriates and were even invited to their dinner parties and were very comfortable with our social life. This presented a problem as the local technicians noticed this friendship and comments were made about my relationship with the English contingent of the company and even my relatives warned me that that it could have social repercussions. The country was going through a political upheaval of racial divisions which were continuing for many years after Trinidad's independence from the UK to become a Republic within the British Commonwealth in 1962.

Life continued on for a few months with me being out between 7 am and 4 pm each day. My wife and baby daughter acclimatised well and fitted well into the family, and we also joined a local Presbyterian Church which was built in honour of my grandfather who was a lay preacher.

Despite many attempts, we never found any suitable accommodation. This became more urgent when we discovered that my wife was pregnant with our second child. I was able to make a significant contribution to the running of the tracking station and was also involved in a few solutions to problems. I was well on the way to being accepted as a suitable candidate to take over the leadership and management of the tracking station however I had to come to some sort of decision whether I should press further for better conditions and a significant increase in my salary to be able to afford the standard of accommodation I was hoping for or retuning to the UK to the job that was being held open for me. The salary of which was significantly more than Textel offered even accounting for the differences in standard of living between the two countries.

I was a self-made man and had suffered many hardships in England to achieve my qualification as an engineer, and I was determined that I would not be pressurised to accept second best and with the knowledge that I had a back stop when I left the UK. Consequently I gave the company an ultimatum that I would resign my post if some of my demands were not being met. The company's response was negative and after three months in the post I gave in my notice and booked our return flight on 'Early Bird' with British Airways to return in May to retake up my post at British Telecom by the 1st of June 1972.

The remaining time in Trinidad we enjoyed time with my family and my wife got on well with her sisters in law and my cousin with whom we were still living as they all had young children too. She was able to fully appreciate what life in Trinidad was like and to this day is glad of the experience she had when we were there even if it was only for six months which boded well for when we retuned for holidays with the family in later years.

The children of my cousin liked playing with baby Sara who was now approaching her first birthday which all we celebrated in true Trini style with all my brothers and their families. Sara loved the Indian music on the local Indian

T.V. station and liked to sing along in her own way. The maid would chatter to her in Hindi and we are sure her first words were in that language.

The neighbour next door had a swimming pool and often invited us to come over and enjoy a swim which we did with my cousin's children. When the heat died down after 4 pm, we took short walks around the locality and once the guard dog managed to get out of the gate before we closed it, he followed us which set all the dogs in the district barking as we went. Needless to say we made sure he did not do it again. All around we were surrounded by sugar cane fields and at harvest time the harvesters set the cane a light to burn off the leaves to make it easier to cut, unfortunately the burnt embers would blow all over the garden and house causing quite a mess. My cousin had a lovely garden with tropical fruit trees.

Often one would see bright green iguanas dash across the lawn. In the house, there were the resident geckos which would hide behind ornaments and pictures on the walls. They earned their keep by eating some of the mosquitos. Birds visiting the garden were colourful and all had their distinctive calls like the kiskadee calling out his name over and over again.

Life in the tropics is very different to the UK and once one has acclimatised it can be very pleasant. Strangely enough as I left home early, worked in air conditioning at the tracking station and returned as it was getting cooler I found the weekends a bit too hot whilst my wife and daughter were fine as they were at home all day and had adapted to the climate.

As the time grew closer to when we were to leave, we were invited to a reception given in honour of the Cable and Wireless managing director. We met and spoke with him and my wife mentioned that her father was an accountant at Cable and Wireless headquarters in London. At the time the company were making redundancies, and her father thought he would be one of those heading for redundancy and we hoped he would be retired on favourable grounds and mentioned this to the director.

We later found out that he was promoted to chief clerk grade before being made redundant. This meant that his pension was higher that it would have been had he been on his previous grade. We are sure that the word in the managing director's ear helped his cause. As he was only 52 years old, he turned to writing books about his favourite hobby of antique clocks. He had several books published and was acknowledged as an expert in this field.

Overall the decision to return to Trinidad was not too much of a disaster as I had fulfilled my dream as a qualified electronic engineer and in retrospect returning back to England proved to be the right decision for my family and my career advancement. I had learnt a few lessons about life one of which was that it is better to try and fail than not to try at all. Philosophically I learnt that the world does not owe you a living but you have to work for it. I stood up for my rights and refused to be pushed into a corner but at the same time one has to weigh up the pros and cons of one's actions. Luckily I had not burnt my bridges and was confident that I would be able to return to continue collecting nuggets in the city which legend says is paved with gold which I found true but had to work very hard to find it.

Chapter 12
A New Start in the UK

We said goodbye to the family and flew back to the UK with just two suit cases as we had sold the furniture and other belongings that we had shipped to Trinidad, thinking that we would need them for our new life. As we had rented out our house for one year to apprentices from Ford Motor Company in Dagenham until December 1972, we went to live with my wife's recently widowed grandfather in North London. One of the first things I did next day was to go to a car dealer in Kingsway London to purchase a car for cash in American dollars. The sales man was surprised that I thought that one could come into a show room and purchase a car off the shelf. When he explained to me that first of all we had to sort out finance and decide on the specifications of the car like type and colour then place an order followed by ordering the car which would take about three months, I was so desperate to have some form of transport which I was denied when in Trinidad that I pointed out to the sales man that there was a car in the show room which suited my specification and I was prepared to purchase that one as I had cash in my pocket. The salesman nearly fell over backwards in shock but when I explained my circumstances and my predicament the sale of a brand new Ford Fiesta at the cost of £950 was agreed. He immediately set about arranging registering the car, the insurance and the road tax. This was a record by any means because I was able to buy a brand new car and drive it home on the same day. My wife was very surprised when I turned up and even the next door neighbour told me that I was lucky to do this in one day as he had been waiting three months for a similar car.

In the meantime, my wife, who was thirty three weeks pregnant with our second child, went to register the family with a GP and was told by the doctor that as she had had a normal delivery with our first child and because of the shortage of hospital beds it would have to be a home delivery. I had two weeks to settle back into the UK before I returned to the same job that was reserved for me at headquarters in London of British Telecom by the 1st of June. During this time we resettled easily in life back in the UK and with my wife's grandad 'Poppa'. He welcomed us and allowed us to decorate and prepare a room in time for delivery of the new baby. He even allowed us to purchase a second-hand fridge as being 'old school' up till this time he had managed perfectly well without one. It was just as well that we were booked for a home delivery as the baby arrived early and after a very brief labour and straight forward delivery our second daughter Rebecca Elizabeth arrived weighing 5lb and 12 ounces. Her great grandfather was so pleased to have a baby in the house especially as my wife was his only grandchild and it also helped him recover from his bereavement. We also found a local church nearby where we worshipped until we returned to our home in December.

I was welcomed when I returned to the office to take up my post and even sat at the same desk with all my files of the various jobs I was involved in and I fell back easily into to the job as though I had only been away a week. Soon afterwards I was sent to Goon Hilly Downs Tracking Station to do some experimental work which involved wiring into the system a circuit which I had designed and constructed. This required the assistance of a technician and I was allocated one of the technicians to wire in the circuit and test the system. When he turned up to my surprise, it was one of the Cable and Wireless technicians who had resigned from British telecom and re-joined the company after being made redundant by Cable and Wireless in Trinidad which was where I had last seen him. He later told me that he had sold up his property in London and on return, because the price of property had inflated so much that he could not afford to buy a house and was living in a caravan. I jokingly mentioned that that whilst he was an expatriate in Trinidad he had lived in luxury with a servant and a gardener whilst I could not afford my own home and had to live with relatives. He said that he was surprised that I had gone through those difficulties, the consequence of which was my resigning my post with Textel and returning to the UK. It was surprises on both sides as the tables had turned in my favour. He also told me that his wife was the daughter of one of the richest business men in Trinidad whom he met there and married. She was not used to living in a caravan in a cold climate as she was used to luxury. However, we got the job completed and the experiment was successful and was later implemented into the system. I was also able to recommend a solution to problems we had at Goon Hilly as it was the same problems we were having at the tracking station in Trinidad which I was able to resolve.

I was now in a position to apply for an interview for enhancement from an assistant executive engineer to executive engineer for which I was successful. I gained further experience in the field of satellite communications and I was given day release to do a course, a Master's Degree course at the University of Surrey. At this point in my career and life, I was not as hungry and ambitious as in previous years and unfortunately did not complete that course.

Chapter 13
Executive Chartered
Engineer and Family

On my promotion to executive engineer, I was transferred to system X a digital telephone system working on the development of digital transmission and mobile phones. I rapidly gained experience at high management level and was on one of the teams to regularly attend meetings with GEC and Plessy collaborating with these companies in the research and development of digital systems. I had many intensive courses at the training college in Staffordshire. I also started a master's degree course at Hertfordshire University on a day release basis. During that time we had a third daughter Vanessa Anne and due to family pressures I could not cope with the course and had to give it up.

However, I sat the council of Institution of Electronic and Electrical Engineers exam for which I was successful and within a short period I was elected a member of the Institute of Electronic and Electrical Engineers. I could now add to my name C.Eng. (Chartered Engineer) M.I. E.E. (Member of the Institute of Electronic and Electrical Engineers). I continued collecting golden nuggets and we had another jewel in the crown when our son Adrian Reuben John was born in 1979.

During those years my salary was increasing more than I hoped for and so was the number of my family so it was decided that we either moved to a larger property or extended by using the spare land we had at the side of the property. As we liked where we lived, we decided on the latter. After gaining planning permission, we extended the kitchen, sitting room, a new bedroom and a playroom. To meet the cost I extended my mortgage and based on the increase in my salary I was well able to meet the cost.

All the children went to a local primary school and as parents we joined the Parent Teachers Association and I was the Social Secretary for 12 years. I was able to afford at least a month's holiday every year and one of the highlights of my children growing up was an annual trip to a caravan site on a farm in Wales near the coastal town of Tenby. We have many happy memories of going there eight years running. The children often talk about the fun times we had on the beach near the farm which was only accessible from the farmer's field via a steep cliff climb, where we caught prawns at low tide and cooked them on a "Primas" stove. We also built fires from driftwood and enjoyed the beach to ourselves as evening drew in. It often rained as it tends to in Wales and the campsite was a non-commercial type with only basic facilities and our caravan only had cold running water and the shower block and toilets were across the field and one of the jobs I did not enjoy was emptying the chemical toilet every morning. Even so there were compensations, the beautiful scenery, plenty of space to fly kites and play ball games. Star gazing was amazing as with no artificial lights you could see the constellations we also witnessed a meteorite storm. Our caravan was next to a family who went there year after year and the children enjoyed each other's company. As the children grew older we had holidays overseas during the Easter break including Malta, Crete and Majorca.

All the children were doing very well at primary and the older two at the local secondary girl's school. They showed great potential and starting making arrangement for their further education. Sara had a desire to become a radiographer and Rebecca wanted to be a teacher. Our youngest daughter liked mathematics and the teachers praised her ability in that field. Our son Adrian required extra tuition by myself to bring him up to an acceptable standard in academic subjects but he had musical skill and played the trumpet and drums for the school music group. He was also a good sportsman especially at cricket as a batsman and wicket keeper, and he played for the school and the local team. He was sent away for a week where cricket bats were made and came home with his own professionally made bat. We were told that this company made bats for famous cricketers not only for English cricketers but also other commonwealth countries including the West Indies and Australia. Later Adrian passed three A levels even though he had a shaky start in education and went on to do a degree in Medical Electronics. The three girls also had advanced education, Sara at University College Hospital to become a radiographer. Rebecca went to Canterbury and did a degree in education and went into primary school teaching and Vanessa got a first-class honour in mathematics and economics.

I continued to be involved with the schools and at one point I was elected to be a governor of the Frances Bardsley Secondary girl's school.

Chapter 14
Four Jewels in Our Crown

We were blessed with four beautiful children and by now we had extended our home even more by adding an additional bedroom. Everything was going smoothly until British Telecom was privatised and there were lots of cost-cutting measures being taken including several departments out of London moving to the provinces where office space was much cheaper. Several departments were being relocated to Swindon and the research headquarters was relocated to Martlesham in Suffolk. I was given opportunity to move to Swindon and was given a week in that town staying in a hotel paid for by the company in order for myself and other members of our staff to help us to make the decision as to where we preferred to be relocated.

At that time, two daughters were at university and our third daughter was in the middle of her GCSE course and that would mean that our family would be separated, and only Adrian would be with us. This was unthinkable and untenable and once again I had another dilemma similar to the one I had in Trinidad all those years ago. The decision now was to accept a redundancy package of a full pension enhanced by six years and a lump sum based on the number of years that I had worked for the company. This package was offered to those approaching 50 years old because it was beneficial for them to get their pension immediately rather than waiting until 60 years of age. One of the recommendations by the city gurus now that BT was quoted on the stock exchange was to start cost cutting by reducing the numbers of staff. A figure of 140,000 senior staff was to be axed. This was due to start of implementation of the new digital system which was now researched and developed and no longer required such high staffing levels. The other motivation was to benefit the share-holders which included me as staff were allocated shares and also given opportunity to purchase shares at a great discount as to what they were quoted on the stock exchange.

I had six months to go before I would qualify for the package and was given the option to move to Martlesham or to accept redundancy when I was fifty in March 1991. I had serious discussions with my wife and after weighing up the pros and cons of disrupting my family or continuing with BT I decided to accept the package. I always wanted to teach mathematics, and I had done some research and found out that 50 years old was the cut-off point for stating a post graduate certificate in education. I had a private discussion with the head of the department and explained to him the position and because he was under pressure to drastically reduce his staff he informally allowed me to start at university in September 1990 until March 1991 on full pay. It seems that I was born with a gold spoon in my mouth because during that time there was a great need for science and maths teachers and the government was offering £1800 a year as a sweetener to tempt people to take up teaching mathematics as a profession. Also in addition to all these goodies coming my way I won a scholarship from the Institution on Electrical and Electronic Engineers of £1000 in payment for my progress as a mature student every three months for my report on my progress on the course.

I started the course in September 1990 by doing two weeks at the local primary school where all my children had attended and I had been the social secretary of the PTA and as such was well known by the staff members. During that time three of us in the family were at university and looking back now it was quite a brave decision I made. The course at the Institute of Education at London University started in October and because the campus was not far from my office in the City the season ticket which I had paid for by the company lasted until March therefore I had no travel expenses. In addition to this, I was able to use the company's canteen as I was still a member of the staff. All these additional benefits mounted up to a great deal as there was no disruption to my budgeting and even though I had to support two children at university one doing A levels and the youngest preparing for his GCSEs.

In March 1991, I officially resigned my post at BT and my income from £30,000/Year as an executive engineer to a university student earning nothing but started getting the company pension. However, to my surprise I got a letter from the BT personnel department that I had one month's leave outstanding and was sent a cheque for one month's pay. All this was added grist to the mill and I knew that there was someone looking after me because from the time I had landed in Southampton in 1961 apart from the two years hard graph the nuggets of 22 carat gold kept rolling in.

Chapter 15
Holiday Home and DIY Skills

I retired for the second time from my teaching profession in 1999 due to deterioration in my ankle for which I had an arthrodesis, this is basically fusing of the joint, enabling walking without pain. It took me six months to recover fully and regain my mobility.

Over the years I developed DIY skills including plumbing, decorating, carpentry, tiling, electrical work, bricklaying and even installing double glazed windows. These skills became useful when we purchased a holiday home in Norfolk with the intention of using it as a bolt hole during the periods we were not traveling to fulfil my other ambition which was to see the world. The property is a detached bungalow which needed modernising and complete redecoration. The first task was to double glaze all the windows and doors. This was before the government introduced 'Fensa' regulations. We also decided to re-clad the facia boards and soffits. This was a mammoth task, but my wife and I did the fitting using a company called Screwfix to supply the materials. All one had to do was to supply them with the correct window and door measurements. This took about two months to complete and the task was made easier by the merit of the property being a bungalow. Our attention then turned to retiling the bathroom and refitting the kitchen with new cabinets. We then set about redecorating the entire house including repapering the walls and ceilings and emulsion painting in colours to our own taste. The central heating system was updated by a local plumber which was the only expense of labour on the entire project. I had a bit of a set back to my health when I needed a triple bypass to alleviate a heart condition but this together with my ankle operation gave me a new lease of life.

During the Covid 19 pandemic lockdown B&Q designed a new kitchen and we employed a fitter, electrician and plumber but I was able to complete the tiling and decorating. Since the rubbish tip was closed during lockdown we had to dispose of all the packaging by burning it after discussing our plan with the neighbours. The alternative was to hire a skip but that would block the drive for at least a month. Then we set about improving the garden by laying new paths and constructing a patio. I was adept at using tools including an electric hedge trimmer to trim the beech hedge surrounding the garden.

Over the years we outgrew our three bedroomed semi-detached family home so we started extending rather than move home. Our first extension was in 1974 and consisted of extending the kitchen, lounge and building a garage attached to the house. The second extension involved converting the garage into a playroom and building a new garage at the end of the garden. Our third venture was to build a room above the play room and remove the wall between the toilet and the bathroom to enlarge the bathroom. More recently we had a loft conversion which consisted of an en-suite bedroom.

During these constructions I was able to use my DIY skills to replace most of the downstairs windows with double glazing, convert the greenhouse into a kitchenette adding a shower and toilet to the playroom making it into an en-suite bedroom. I added two porches one at the front of the house and brick built another one at the back of the house and have since retiled the kitchen bathroom and toilets.

More recently we inherited the property of my wife's parents and after having it double glazed I refurbished the entire house including wallpapering and painting. B&Q designed a kitchen for which we employed a fitter but I did the plumbing and tiling and flooring. We redesigned the garden back and front and more recently we resurfaced the drive to the garage with loose chippings. The final job at my wife's parent's house was to have block pave the frontage and the pavement dropped by the council.

Chapter 16
Foreign Travels

We then started our foreign travel to achieve my long held childhood ambition to see the world and experience other cultures and foods. The places we went to either by way of cruising or touring by coach, air travel or by our own means of transport.

We had many adventurous holidays which started when we saw a 12 day trip to China advertised including a boat trip on the Yangtze River before the dam was built so we saw the three gorges before they were submerged by rising water caused by the dam. We also walked on the Great Wall, saw the forbidden city in Beijing also seeing Tiananmen Square and danced with the local people when we were in Chongqing, we then flew to Wuhan, now infamous for the start of the 2020 2021 Corona virus pandemic, and saw the animal market with lots of weird, caged animals for sale for human consumption.

The following year we went to Australia where we stayed in a self-catering apartment on the coast at Trinity Beach near Cairns for a month. During that time we took a train trip to Sydney along the Gold coast. The ticket allowed us to get off at various stages and stay in hotels along the way and re-join the train which sometimes ran two days later. We stopped one night in Brisbane which is a beautiful city.

Eventually we arrived in Sydney had a boat trip around the harbour and saw the famous opera house and the harbour bridge. We took a bus ride to the famous Bondi Beach and were quite underwhelmed by it after hearing so much about it. We visited Sydney botanical gardens where we saw hundreds of fruit bats hanging asleep on the trees. The return journey was not so straight forward as a tropical cyclone had hit Cairns in our absence and the rail track was damaged north of Townsville. The railway company put us up in a hotel there for two nights including all meals. This gave us the opportunity to visit Magnetic Island with its amazing vegetation and wildlife; we even saw a cane toad the size of a dinner plate! Queensland Rail flew us back to Cairns as the railway track would take several weeks to repair. We were a bit anxious about getting back as we could not contact the apartments and wondered if they were still standing after the cyclone. All our return tickets were in the apartment safe but as it turned out it was only that the phone lines were down and a few coconut trees around the apartment gardens.

Also during our time in Queensland we took a train into the interior called the Savannah Lander line with about 20 other tourist passengers some of whom were Australians. It was a four day journey up onto the plateau behind Cairns through mango and coffee plantations. At one point, the train stopped and we were asked to get off to clear the line of sand that had blown onto the track armed with brooms and shovels! We stopped at an old mining town that had long since ceased working but which still retained a small population centred on the saloon where we sampled local beer. The last port of call was a cattle ranch of huge proportions were the owner said the way they herded the cows was by helicopter. Another adventure was to visit a town where the indigenous people or Aborigines lived called Karunda. It was accessed by cable car over a forested hill. Whilst there we stayed in a backpacker's hostel which was primitive by anyone's estimation!

Amazingly the owner was from our home town of Hornchurch having emigrated many years previously with his parents. The tour included a conducted walk into the surrounding tropical forest with an aboriginal guide who showed us which plants were used for medicine or even leaves which could be a substitute for soap. He talked of the old days when each young man had to go 'walk about' for three months as an initiation rite living by his wits and killing game to eat. He told us about the terrifying bird called a cassowary which could disembowel a man with one kick of its huge talons. This tradition is not possible now as the Australian government has put protection orders on all the wild life and no one could survive without hunting for food. To round off the tour we went to a theatre show of aboriginal dancing and comedy chat where they took the micky out of the European Australians.

Chapter 17
Experiencing Other Cultures
in the World

We then continued our foreign travel to achieve my long held childhood ambition to see the world and experience other cultures and foods. The places we went to either by way of cruising or touring by coach, air travel or by our own means of transport.

Egypt – January 2004

In January 2004, we went on a cruise down the Nile from Luxor to the Aswan dam. The tour started by exploring the 'valley of the kings' and seeing the inside of the tombs with their ornate murals. The guide was an Egyptian archaeologist who had extensive knowledge of the area.

Most of the tombs had been raided by robbers many years before so there were no human remains or artefacts left. As we sailed down the Nile, either side was covered in lush vegetation. We stopped at various villages and witnessed the life style of the Egyptian people and you could imagine them as the ancient inhabitants as their life style probably had not changed in thousands of years. We were taken to the ruins of the village of the tomb makers and a local guide explained that after they had dug the king's tombs they were forced to remain in their village to prevent them telling the secrets of the royal tombs. We sailed as far as the Aswan dam and viewed the huge lake Nasser from the dam wall. We had a ride on felucca a traditional Egyptian sailing vessel and saw various temples dedicated to ancient Egyptian gods. It was a very memorable cruise and we made friends with a couple who invited us to stay at their Spanish holiday home. After the cruise, we had a week's stay in Luxor at a luxury hotel.

We thought that a trip to Egypt would not be complete without seeing the pyramids and the sphinx at Giza near Cairo so we made enquiries at Luxor railway station and booked a night sleeper train to Cairo. The night of our departure for Cairo the station platform was heaving with people and their luggage as unknown to us it was the feast of Abraham's sacrifice of his son Ishmael according to Islamic tradition. The

9.30 pm train pulled into the station and on our ticket it said 9.30 pm train to Cairo so we duly boarded and looked for our cabin number only to our consternation to find a family already in occupation. We spoke to the conductor and he looked at our tickets and pointed out a very small letter 'b' and said we were on the 9.30 'a' train by which time the train was already moving. "Don't worry," he said. "I will radio the train behind and drop you off at the next station and it will pick you up there." At Dendera, we dismounted the train and sat on a bench. It was pitch black and rather cold but being reassured by the conductor that we would be picked up we waited as instructed. Suddenly out of the darkness two soldiers armed with A.K. 47s accosted us and asked what are we doing here at this time of night to which we replied we are waiting for a train. "No trains stop here," they said and we assured them that we would be picked up. He demanded to see our passports to which request we complied; no one argues with a rifle pointed at you! Just then a large light appeared as a train approached with the conductor leaning out of a window calling our name. It stopped and we thankfully climbed aboard. Phew, we were at last on our way to Cairo. We were shown to our compartment and served with an airline type meal. Later the steward converted the compartment into sleeping accommodation and we settled in to bed.

On arrival at Cairo, we were hit by the noise and bustle of that city. We were beset by taxi drivers wanting to drive us. We finally chose one and negotiated a price and asked to be taken to the Cairo museum. It is a magnificent building full of Egyptian artefacts including the fantastic sarcophagus of Tutankhamun and the treasures found in his tomb. We stared at the mummified remains of an ancient Pharaoh thinking that in life we would never been allowed so close to someone who was considered a god.

Later we looked for a taxi to take us to Giza to see the pyramids. After negotiating what we thought a fair price, we drove off but entered a village with piles of sheep skins still blooded from the kill. The driver said,

"I take you to my friend who has camels; he will take you to see the pyramids." We were a bit taken aback but thought this could be fun. Never having ridden a camel before getting on was quite an experience as the beast first raises its rear legs and you think you are going to fall over its head then it raises its front legs and you are up hanging on for dear life! All aboard and it was off into the dessert I was trying to video with one hand and clutching the reins with the other as the camel trotted along the sand dunes and after a two hour trek there were the pyramids in all their splendour. Wow what a site! We thought we were with Lawrence of Arabia. On the way back, the camel owner and the camel leader demanded their baksheesh (tip) and since he had control of the speed of the camel we had no choice but to meet his demand.

Back in the village all the camel owners relatives were demanding tips too. We caught the overnight train back to Luxor and arrived at 5am and were picked up by a pre-arranged taxi. There were three of us in the back and I sat in the front and to my astonishment he stopped in the middle of a roundabout and asked me to move over so that his friend, a learner driver, who he was teaching could get in. Our friends did not want to have any of it and threatened to get out and not pay as it was too dangerous so the driver relented and took us back to the hotel. That driver stayed with us for the week and he showed us more of the local sights not usually visited by tourists. During that week we went to the 'son et luminaire' show at the temple at Karnack which is one of the main highlights of Luxor. From our hotel room, we were mesmerised by the sun setting over the Nile. By now, we had well and truly caught the travel bug. Soon after we arrived home we booked a holiday to Sri Lanka.

Sri Lanka – December 2004

At Colombo airport, we were surprised that all arriving passengers had their luggage opened by a team of persons wearing rubber gloves who rummaged through everything thoroughly before allowing us to leave the airport. Later we realised that this was due to the ongoing tension between the two main groups of people in Sri Lanka, the Tamils and the Singhalese and the threat of terrorist attacks. We met the tour guide outside were immediately hit by the tropical heat and the sight of exotic vegetation. We were driven by coach to our hotel in Negombo which was right next to the beach on the Indian Ocean coast. The next morning the guide went through the itinerary of optional tours which included a visit to the Pinnawala elephant sanctuary. That was something not to be missed and when we arrived there we were amazed to see so many elephants which for various reasons needed special care. There were retired working elephants which could not be released into the wild, orphaned baby elephants which needed hand rearing and some who had been injured by traps or even bombs in the jungle another reminder of the political unrest in Sri Lanka. We saw the elephants taken to the river to bathe and their carers got in too and scrubbed their charges. For most of the holiday, we arranged our own trips one of which was to take the local train to the capital city Colombo for sightseeing and shopping. In a garden park, the was an escaped cobra belonging to a snake charmer and local children were screaming but I think it was a set up as the escapee was soon safely back in its basket.

Later we were told that these snakes usually have their fangs removed but one can ever be too careful! We joined another couple and took a taxi to the inland town of Kandy where there is the fabled temple of the tooth which is said to be one belonging to the Buddha himself.

One morning we took a tuk-tuk ride into the town of Negombo to visit the fruit and vegetable market. Out in the street which was thronging with people and was so busy with traffic one had to be very vigilant not to be knocked down.

Suddenly we were approached by a policeman and we wondered if we had transgressed any rules. However, it turned out that he just wanted to talk to us as we were obviously tourists. He told us that he was a Tamil, but also a Christian, and would we like to attend his church on the following Sunday to which we readily agreed. He said he would send a tuk-tuk to pick us up from our hotel and on Sunday morning we set off for a very moving experience. At the church, there were both Tamils and Singhalese and when we walked in we were noticed immediately and welcomed. The service commenced and was conducted in three languages Tamil, Singhalese and in our honour English. This took a long time but we really appreciated the service.

Towards the end a young man of not more than 16 got up to speak. He said that he felt that some event of serious nature was going to take place soon and that we should fast and pray about it. It was only three weeks later that the Boxing Day tsunami hit the coasts of Thailand and Sri Lanka causing mass destruction and deaths. Did this young man have divine inspired foresight of this devastating event? We will never know as we left Sri Lanka two weeks before that occurred and realise that by the grace of God we were saved as our hotel was in the direct path of the killer wave and we would have been at breakfast in the beach side restaurant at the time it hit.

Turkey – November 2005

We wanted to see the places of the churches mentioned in the book of Revelation and parts of the Ottoman Empire. We flew from Heathrow to Istanbul and spent a few days visiting various mosques including the famous blue mosque with its six minarets also known as Hagia Sophia.

This was once a Christian church and one can still see where the Christian art had been obliterated. We also visited the Suleiman mosque which is an imperial Ottoman mosque located on the third hill of Istanbul. The mosque was commissioned by Suleiman the Magnificent in the year 1550 We saw the Topkapi Palace which housed lots of treasures and also was the residence of the sultan with all of his harem. We went on a boat ride up the Bosphorus strait to the Black Sea and were able to walk across the bridge that connected Europe to Asia.

We then set off by coach to Troy and climbed on a reconstruction of the famous Trojan horse. We visited the seven churches of the revelation also known as the seven churches of the apocalypse which are the seven major churches of early Christianity. Our first stop was Pergamon. It was raining with thunder and lightning and it reminded us of what the Bible said of this church that it was where Satan had his throne. Then we went to Sardis Philadelphia Smyrna and Ephesus and saw where St Paul addressed the crowds in the amphitheatre there. The last church we visited was at Laodicea. Unfortunately the island of Patmos, where John had his vision of the Revelation, was not on the itinerary because it is a Greek island.

A Coach Trip Round Eastern Europe – 2006

The following year we went on a coach trip to Eastern Europe starting in Budapest Hungary and had a night cruise on the blue Danube and also saw the shoes sculpture to commemorate the mass drowning of Jews before going to Austria where we saw the palaces and stately buildings of Vienna and the Lipizzaner stallions at the famous Spanish riding school where the breed of horses known as Lipizzaner trace their lineage back to the sixteenth century. From there, we went Prague in the Czech Republic. We visited the Wenceslas Square, the Prague castle and the astronomical clock first installed in 1410 making it the third oldest clock and only functional one in the world. We ended our tour in Warsaw Poland and also visited Gdansk a beautiful city located on the Baltic sea. We saw one of the best pipe organs in the world in the Oliwa Cathedral and listened to an organ concert. The Rococo organ consists of 8000 pipes and many moving elements. Pope John Paul the first non-Italian pope since 1522 who was elected in 1978 came from Gdansk.

Chapter 18
The Arctic Circle and North Cape in Norway by Car

We spent three weeks motoring in our 'Rotel' (Our car converted into a Hotel on wheels) in Norway staying at the many camp sites along the way towards the North Cape inside the Arctic Circle to see the midnight sun. This may seem an impossible trip to make by car but with careful planning it proved to be relatively easy.

It took me a few months planning the journey and the first important fact I discovered was that the Norwegians start their summer holiday from 21st of June each year and that the roads would be busy after that date and all campsites would be fully booked. Consequently on this knowledge I planned the journey to start in early in June and end before the holiday season. The next important issue was the dealing with the possibility of breakdowns but this was soon resolved by joining the Viking Breakdown Association who offered the same conditions as the RAC or AA including provision of transport to your doorstep if it was necessary offered at their highest level of membership. It also had all the petrol stations marked on the map they provided.

We learnt that one can camp freely by the roadside once one went north of Tromso so we equipped ourselves with all the necessary camping gear and all the necessary sleeping comforts. I removed the back seat of our Mondeo car which left sufficient level space for a double blow up bed and enough space in the seat wells to store three weeks of tinned food including dried potato, pasta and rice and anything that could be mixed with boiling water in plastic storage boxes as we knew that food in Norway was extremely expensive. We also supplemented our diet with a daily multivitamin tablet. We purchased an ingeniously designed tent called a Caranex which was basically an extension to the car in the form of tent attached over the tailgate providing sufficient space for cooking and sitting. A roof rack transported the tent and other equipment such as our folding picnic table which also had integral chairs.

We set off in the early hours morning of the 7th of June 2005 to catch the ferry from Newcastle to Bergen and we booked a cabin for the twenty two hour trip (the cabin cost us an extra £20 over the fare of £100). As we left the port we felt a sense of excitement leaving the coast of England behind for the adventure that we had dreamed of for a quite a few years. We saw porpoises following the ship which added to that feeling of anticipation. The next morning we approached Bergen with all the different coloured buildings on the waterfront it looked like somewhere from a fairy tale. The ship docked and we drove off the landing stage and headed for our first destination a town called Voss. The map showed one main roads one could not get lost.

The town of Voss had that same fairy tale feel and we visited the thirteenth-century wooden church. We booked into a three star campsite near the base of the Tvinnofoss waterfall which had a 150 metre drop. The camp site had first class facilities including washing machines tumble driers showers, toilets and a kitchen. This was the standard of camp sites throughout the journey. The roar of the waterfall could be heard all night. As it was June there was hardly any darkness so we were up early the next morning to continue our epic journey. Leaving Voss we climbed Vikafjell where the scenery was completely white and at one point it even started to snow! We descended to Vik the small town which gave its name to the most famous of Norwegians-the Vikings. Standing above the town is the timbered Hopperstad stave church built in 1150.

Continuing to Vagnes we sailed on a ferry over Sognefjord to Balestrand (it cost us 103N.K. – £10 for us and the car) then we took the road westwards. The following day Forde and the Huldrefoss falls beckoned to the north. Passing through the town of Stryn we continued to the ferry at Standa and camped overnight.

Awakening the next day we headed towards Andalsens. Like a slender thread through the snow the road led to the summit of the 3000 ft. pass where walls of snow cleared from the road towered 12 ft. either side of the road, fortunately there was no oncoming traffic. Dropping quickly down the hillside and carefully negotiating eleven hairpin bends, crossing a spectacular waterfall we stopped to view the Trillvigan mountain wall stretching some 5000 feet up from the valley floor. The quality of the scenery continued undiminished as we travelled north east to Trondheim. Where saw the magnificent Cathedral with its fantastic stone carved frontage. This was the place where on a steep sided road there was a devise to aid one transporting one's bike or a child's pram up to the top costing 1 Norwegian Krona (NK) This was the place for starting our attempt to reach the Polar Circle.

Driving out of the suburbs of Trondheim we passed through one of the best known places in Norway – the small town of Hell so with many others we can say we have been to Hell and back! Edging further north we reached the Arctic Circle at about 3.30 pm. after having driven for six days and covering nine hundred miles. The line of latitude that is the Arctic Circle is marked by a series of four foot high pillars surmounted by five iron rings forming a globe. Standing on the Saltfjell Plateau some 2000 ft. above sea level there was deep snow lying all around and beside the road but it was warm with the sun light reflecting off the snow. Everywhere there were stacks of loose memorial stones made by people who had been there so we too built one for us. We promptly went inside the tourist shop to send cards to friends and relatives with the Arctic Circle stamp to prove that we had crossed the Arctic Circle.

Having crossed the line we headed towards Norway's most northerly point the North Cape to witness the midnight sun crossing the northern horizon. After camping by a raging river, our first night inside the Arctic Circle, we set off for the Nord Kapp a journey which would take another five days and 620 miles. On the way, there we visited the beautiful city of Tromso with its glass cathedral shaped like an iceberg. By now, the weather was quite hot and the sun shone day and night around the horizon rather than overhead. We now benefited from the blackout curtains we had made to fit over the car windows and wind screen so we could sleep at night. Once we were inside the Arctic Circle one can camp by the road side which we did near rivers and waterfalls the water of which is so pure one could safely drink it. Also there were toilets with heating that were very clean with all facilities which were located along the route in the wild to be used by visitors. We washed in the river water and filled our water containers.

North of Tromso the route traversed bleak moorland with the rapidly melting snow the ground was very boggy. We camped in a layby and saw evidence of moose having passed that way (tracks and droppings.) Continuing our journey we had to stop to allow a herd of hundreds of reindeer to cross the road. We also saw an arctic fox half way through its moulting of its winter coat and an arctic hare.

In Finnmark, Norway's most northerly county, we came across a Sarni community (the nomadic people from Lapland who do not recognise international borders.) They make their living selling reindeer skins, horns and artefacts made from these.

The Sarni people wear tunics of bright blue and embroidered in red and gold over trousers of reindeer skin and furry boots.

About five miles before the North Cape centre there was a toll gate and to our astonishment we had to pay 21N.K. each! The attendant mentioned that clear sky meant we would get a good view of the sun and this helped to appease us of the shock of the expensive entrance fee. Finally after a steep climb we reached the 1000 ft. high cliffs of the Nord Kapp or North Cape ten days and one thousand seven hundred miles from Bergen. The sun was shining brightly but the wind was blowing at gale force which made it feel like ten degrees. However later in the evening the wind abated and we watched with awe as the sun descended towards the horizon at midnight without setting and then ascended again. This phenomenon was something we had always wanted to experience. It is so special that everyone should attempt to witness it. The site is heavily commercialised and there were hundreds of tourists from all parts of the world. We were allowed to camp there free of charge and after setting up our Caranex in a less windy part we were surrounded by a group of longhaired leather clad Dutch motor cyclists. We were a bit worried at first but then they invited us to join them for food and drinks. That was another experience that we will never forget and learnt that you cannot judge people by their appearance.

We returned to Bergen and camped there for two nights. We took a bus to the city centre, the conductor thought my wife was my career and as I was a pensioner we both went free and spent a day doing the usual tourist things before sailing back to Newcastle for our journey home. We have never experienced a three week holiday with so much spectacular scenery where every camp site and every stopping place provided a feast of breath taking views. This was another golden nugget for my collection.

Chapter 19
Cruising Around the World
Alaska via the Inside Passage

We arrived in Calgary in Canada for a three day coach tour of the Rockies prior to boarding the cruise ship Star Princess at Vancouver. The ship was 16 stories high and accommodated 3000 passengers plus 1000 crew. We were amazed at the luxury aboard and the clientele, most of whom were wealthy Americans and rich retirees from Britain. Although we were on one of the lower deck cabins, that was irrelevant, as all the facilities were available to all and one's dining companions could be from any class. We visited the towns along the so called inside passage and saw huge chunks of ice breaking of the glaciers in Alaska. Whether this was a natural occurrence or the result of global warming the sound of the ice crashing into the sea was like a tremendous clap of thunder and the result was a new iceberg floating by the ship. We saw a few whales spouting in the distance but nothing close up. We flew back from Ankara to Vancouver thence to London. It is amazing to think that the vast Alaskan territory was sold by the Russians to America for the princely sum of $1,000,000!

Hong Kong and the Far East

The following year 2008 we flew to Hong Kong and were amazed as the aircraft seemed to narrowly miss the tops of sky scrapers as we came into land! This area of China is very prosperous and progressive and the place was a dream world for people looking to purchase the latest technology in mobile phones cameras and other techno gadgets.

The first day we were hit by a deluge and were surprised to see ladies with brooms sweeping the water off the pavements. In the modern shops, one was provided with a plastic bag in which to put your umbrella and prevent drips landing on the shop floor which was constantly being mopped. The British certainly left their mark one of which was the gardens at Victoria heights reached by a funicular railway.

We boarded the ship Costa Allegra and sailed to Manilla in the Philippines. The weather was very hot and humid but the people were very friendly and the scenery beautiful. By tradition, a big band with dancers performed a 'send-off' ceremony as we pulled away from shore and headed towards our next destination of Borneo. We were taken to a jungle village. It was pouring with rain and we crossed a river via a rope and wooden slatted bridge which swung from side to side. It was an experience not to miss especially when we were welcomed by the villagers selling their crafts. We called into Brunei and saw the Sultan's magnificent palace. He is one of the richest people in the world and supplies all the people's electricity as a means of sharing his wealth.

After leaving Indonesia, we sailed to Singapore. This is a well organised and progressive city and we were amazed how clean the underground railway was compared to the London underground. Eating on the trains is forbidden and strictly observed. You cannot visit Singapore without visiting the famous Raffles Hotel for a Singapore Sling cocktail and we treated ourselves to afternoon tea.

Our next port of call was Saigon in Vietnam now called Ho Chi Minh City. There were hundreds of people on mopeds with multiple passengers and household items balanced on the passenger's heads. Even though there were zebra crossings, no one observed them and we were told just walk across and don't hesitate and they will just ride around you. This was nerve racking but we soon got used to it and survived to tell the tale! Street peddlers were in abundance and bartering was the norm and we did buy one or two souvenirs including a lovely pearl necklace.

Cruising the South China Sea was very pleasurable and we saw some magnificent sunsets and tasted many types of cuisine on board and on land. Finally back in Hong Kong we visited the local markets before flying back home after a truly enjoyable and unforgettable experience.

Cruises Starting from Tilbury

We live not far from Tilbury docks a port for cruise ships so we took the opportunity to book several cruises from that port.

Round Britain

The ship first sailed up the east coast towards Scotland to Invergarry then on to the Orkney islands and visited the site of Skara Brae located on the bay of Skaill on the west coast of mainland, the largest island in the Orkney archipelago of Scotland. This village dates back to Neolithic times over 5000 years ago. Radio carbon dating suggests that people were living there for around 650 years between 3180 BC and 2500 BC making it older than Stonehenge and the pyramids of Giza. The cruise then took us to Dublin and we took a bus tour of the city but unfortunately the famous Guinness factory was closed!

Chapter 20
Surviving Various Health Issues

I have to thank the NHS for being able to write my memoires today as I had many health issues during my life to date. In 1990, I had just started my teaching career at the age of 5O when I had my first health scare.

Stroke

It was the start of the Easter break and I was not feeling too great. After breakfast, I collapsed and was unable to walk and seemed to be drunk and felt very cold. My son and my wife struggled to get me upstairs to bed and wrapped me in the bed quilt but I still felt extremely cold. My wife thinking that it was probably the 'flu' said that if I was no better this afternoon she would call the doctor. Indeed I was no better and the doctor ordered that I should go to A and E at the local hospital. Doctors there were mystified and questioned me as to my recent travels – was it malaria they thought, when I told them we had only been to France that was discounted. The only way we can tell what it maybe is a head scan they informed me which was performed the next day. In my wife's mind was, "It's a brain tumour," but she said nothing to me.

When my wife visited me on the ward the next day, the doctor said the head scan showed that I had suffered a stroke in the area of the brain controlling balance to which she replied, "Thank goodness," but seeing the puzzled expression on the doctors face she quickly explained that she had thought it was a brain tumour judging from the symptoms. I remained in hospital for a week and spent a further six weeks at home before returning to work. The primary effects were the total loss of my memory of all things mathematical but this gradually returned and after the six weeks I was able to return to teaching maths however with some difficulties remembering certain equations like how to solve quadrilateral equations using the formula. I also struggled to remember certain words and people's names and I still to this day struggle with these two issues and my wife often prompts me when she realises that I am having difficulties.

Arthrodesis of My Right Ankle

I was diagnosed with arterial arteritis in 1998 for which I was prescribed steroids. This medication also helped my painful ankle which was becoming arthritic. As the steroid doses were reduced and the arterial arteritis was cured my ankle became more and more painful to the point that at the end of the day I could hardly walk and eventually I went on sick leave.

In 1999, the doctor referred me to an orthopaedic surgeon who recommended that I have an arthrodesis so that

I could walk without pain. Basically this procedure fixes the ankle in a permanent right angle position. My foot was in plaster for three months. The doctor recommended that I apply for early retirement which I did in the year 2000.

Cardiac Bypass

We continued our travels to China the Far East and Australia. However, in September 2006, I became increasingly breathless when walking any distance and was experiencing tightness in my chest. At a routine health check, the doctor asked me if I had any chest tightness or pain and I replied, "Yes on the way to the surgery." She forthwith sent me to A&E. when there the doctor ordered blood tests to ascertain whether I had had a heart attack and questioned me on my health issues. When he had finished, he admitted me straight away. Two days later I had an angiogram which showed that one coronary artery was completely blocked and two others partially. It was recommended that I stay in hospital until a bed was found for me at the London Chest Hospital. This stay turned out to be seven weeks on ward E 4 at Oldchurch Hospital which was scheduled to be demolished by the end of the year. During that time, I made quite a number of friends and up until today I am still in touch. Because I was in a two bedded room which was used mainly for short stay patients I was able to gain an insight into the lives of people from different walks of life. I met a person who during the 2nd World War who was involved in moving road signs around to confuse any invading forces, a taxi driver who talked about his many exploits, a school master with whom I had much in common and even the linen lady I met on my walks around the hospital to avoid daily anti-coagulant injections. Even the doctors and ambulant patients came into my room for social chats. I made friends with one of the cleaners of Nigerian decent who wanted to be like me able to do crosswords and speak with a BBC accent. I recommended him to go to an elocution evening class and other classes to improve his education. I later found out that he had taken my advice and he had been promoted to the position of Hospital housekeeper in charge of the cleaning staff. I was a popular patient and was allowed to use the nurse's room for showering and enjoyed some privileges from the food trolley. I remembered when I was told a bed was available and an ambulance came to take me to the chest hospital for my operation a guard of honour formed of doctors, nurses, patients, the linen lady, and even the food trolley lady came to wish me all the best. My room was covered in photographs of the nurses, pictures from my grandchildren and various slogans stuck to the walls. The matron saw them and said I was only allowed to do this as the hospital was being demolished in a couple of weeks' time but warned me it would not be allowed in any other hospital! I had a triple coronary bypass and a five day stay in hospital. After three months, we were back on our travels.

Major Bowel Surgery

In January 2007, I had a rectal bleed and immediately made an appointment with my GP Without any hesitation she sent a fax to the newly built Queens Hospital. Two days later I was sent an appointment for a sigmoidoscopy which revealed a suspicious looking tumour from which a biopsy was taken. Two weeks later we received the bad news that it was a carcinoma and would require surgery. All the same we went ahead with our planned holiday to Madeira. We enjoyed the many walks on the island and the warm sunshine. On returning to the UK, we had a date for my operation in March. The anaesthetist was reluctant to give me an anaesthetic as had only had my coronary artery bypass operation three months previously but when I told him we had been walking four or five miles every day on holiday without any problems or breathlessness it was decided that I would be alright to have a general anaesthetic. The operation was successful and no other cancer was found. My recovery was uneventful and no further treatment was necessary except yearly check-up appointments e.g. scans and colonoscopies. I have now been dismissed from this department. All credits to the NHS and the swift action of my GP I will ever be thankful to them and to God for preserving my life.

Prostate Problems

In 2015, after having several episodes of difficulty in passing urine and when my PSA levels were rising the urology consultant at the hospital decided to perform a biopsy of the prostate. The result showed an adeno-carcinoma of the anterior of the prostate at grade 4 level. My wife was with me in the urologist's consulting room which was just as well as I went completely numb and could not concentrate on what he was saying. She listened very carefully and later told me she kept saying to herself I must take in all the doctor is telling us. We saw the consultant's nurse who reassured us that my treatment would start that day with tablets to supress my testosterone levels (prostate tumours are dependent upon this hormone to grow). This would be followed by monthly injections to further reduce testosterone levels. The nurse explained that before any further treatment commenced I would need to have a bone scan to check that the cancer had not spread beyond the prostate. The bone scan was clear so I was referred to the oncology consultant who told me I would need thirty five doses of radiation (radio therapy) to the prostate over a period of seven weeks. Each week day would drive to the hospital for my treatment come home and go to bed for two hours which I am sure helped me to reduce any side effects from the radiation. I prayed to God for healing and on one occasion I distinctly heard his voice saying, "I will heal you, Harry," and I was greatly encouraged. Christmas Eve was the day of my last dose of radio therapy and we enjoyed Christmas dinner with all our children and their spouses, grandchildren and my wife's parents. There were 16 of us around the table and though tired from my ordeal I was over the moon that we were altogether to celebrate.

Two weeks after Christmas a further blood test showed that my PSA level had fallen and subsequent tests every six months showed it fall to barely readable levels. These tests carried on until this year and I have now been dismissed by the oncology team at the hospital. God's promise had been fulfilled!

Bowel Obstruction

I had been in good health until October 2021 when suddenly I was struck down with very severe abdominal pain. I felt faint and nauseous so my wife took by blood pressure which was very low so she said that I should lie down but before we could achieve that my wife told me that I lost consciousness and started to fit. That was when she called 999. The ambulance arrived within 15 minutes and the paramedics examined me. By that time, I had regained consciousness and was able to respond to their questions. They took me to our local hospital Queens in Romford. Once there I was examined by a doctor who ordered X rays and a CT Scan. By now, I was vomiting and was given an injection to relieve this.

Eventually I was admitted to a ward and told it was probably an obstruction of the bowel and that they would try to relieve it with medication. After two days, it was decided to operate and the surgeon removed about 30 centimetres of small bowel and I went back to the ward to recover. Recovery took longer than expected as the bowel stopped functioning. I was fed intravenously and was unable to eat for seven days when eventually things started to move and I was able to eat small amounts of soft food. After being in hospital for a total of 17 days, I was allowed home.

When I saw the surgeon at the outpatients five weeks later, he told me that the obstruction was caused by a rare type of tumour called a neural-endocrine tumour a low grade type of cancer. He said there was no evidence of further cancer in the abdomen but ordered a CT scan of the thorax to check for any other tumours. That was performed in December and the result was clear. I will be seeing the surgeon again in May and am hopeful that all will be alright.

I am now 81 and it has been a long journey to reach this stage of achieving my ambition following my dream from beyond the Dragon's Mouth to the land of milk and money.

Chapter 21
The World Does Not Owe You a Living but You Have to Work for It

This was the philosophy of my mother and father which has passed down to me and all my siblings. No doubt this was based on the fact that they were the products of progressive indentured labourers who had risked everything to travel from Calcutta via the Dragon's Mouth to Port of Spain. In spite of limited education but loads of wisdom, they inspired us all to work hard and aim to progress upwards to higher levels in the hierarchical levels of society. They instilled into us Christian values and importance of education but above all the respect for all human beings whether of any ethnicity, religion or culture. We were all achievers but for some reason I had that extra desire to achieve what my other rich friends were able to do in higher education such as going to university which was the privilege of the wealthy. It proved to me that determination is more powerful than wealth because after many years in England when I returned to my homeland I was able to compare the progress of my well to do friends to my personal success. I returned to my homeland as a chartered engineer and as the manager designate of the Trinidad telephone company of the satellite tracking department. I was the only Trinidadian with satellite tracking expertise following my experience gained working as an executive engineer at the satellite tracking station in Goonhilly in Cornwall in the days of Telstar 1966. In comparison to my other rich friends, only one became a millionaire by re-writing the educational curriculum structuring it to reflect more of the West Indian culture and environment. The others remained at the same level.

From my experience, it is more beneficial to work for what you have because one builds up fortitude, respect for people but above all to be mindful of one's attitude and concern for humanity. The more powerful the wind the stronger the breeze and greater the strength of the branches of the trees. This philosophy has taught me over the years how to be kind to people because I received lots of kindness from people I met on the journey to where I am today. I remember the kindness an Englishman showed me when I was on the production line assembling radios, when I first came to England, he realised that I was not used to manual work and after some conversation he thought I would be more productive further up the line to a job which was more technical in nature than a manual one. I remember the kindness shown to me by a friend from Sri Lanka who offered me accommodation when I was thrown out of my apartment and was homeless for a while.

These memories come back to me time and time again and somehow have carved out the character of my being. Writing a memoir plunges you back into places you may not want to revisit like the opposition and prejudice one had to face from people including my wife's parents when we were courting and the cold evil eye from people in the street. At one point, I was tempted to throw in the towel and return to my homeland. But on reflection when you have a goal you are filled with enthusiasm, obsessions, tastes and weaknesses. And today here am I at age 81 a man who has it all. There is the loving beautiful wife, successful children, all university educated, seven lovely grandchildren, a lovely home including a holiday home and over the years have visited more than 67 countries. Sadly my cruising days and holidays abroad have come to a halt firstly due to Covid but mainly due to the cost of travel insurance. We tried to renew our annual travel insurance in readiness for a Caribbean cruise and because of my age, now 81, and various health issues I was quoted £7,500. My previously booked holiday to Transylvania which was cancelled due to the lockdown would cost me £4500 being in Europe. But we have beautiful beaches in England, green and pleasant Ireland and what I consider little Switzerland in Scotland. We have good education facilities for our children, rain which helps our crops to grow and above all the best National Health Service (NHS) in the world. Looking at the parallel universe I wonder where I would be if my forefathers had not left India gone through the DRAGON'S MOUTH!

The United Kingdom is a beautiful country paved with gold and is a land of MILK AND MONEY to those who think otherwise 'THE WORLD DOES NOT OWE ANYONE A LIVING BUT YOU HAVE TO WORK FOR IT'.

Milton Keynes UK
Ingram Content Group UK Ltd.
UKHW022218181123
432823UK00013B/280

9 781398 495166